Strategic Project Risk Appraisal and Management

Strategic Project Risk Appraisal and Management

ELAINE HARRIS

Routledge
Taylor & Francis Group

LONDON AND NEW YORK

First published 2009 by Gower Publishing

Published 2016 by Routledge
2 Park Square, Milton Park, Abingdon, Oxon OX14 4RN
711 Third Avenue, New York, NY 10017, USA

Routledge is an imprint of the Taylor & Francis Group, an informa business

British Library Cataloguing in Publication Data
Harris, Elaine.
 Strategic project risk appraisal and management. --
 (Advances in project management)
 1. Project management. 2. Risk management.
 I. Title II. Series
 658.4'04-dc22

Library of Congress Cataloging-in-Publication Data
Harris, Elaine.
 Strategic project risk appraisal and management / by Elaine Harris.
   p. cm. -- (Advances in project management)
 Includes bibliographical references and index.
 ISBN 978-0-566-08848-3 (pbk) 1. Risk management. 2. Project management. I. Title.
 HD61.H337 2009
 658.15'5--dc22

                                                                    2009016188

ISBN 13: 978-0-566-08848-3 (pbk)

CONTENTS

LIST OF FIGURES

LIST OF TABLES

ACKNOWLEDGEMENTS

As the preface indicates, this short book has emerged after many years of working with and thinking about strategic project appraisal and risk management. The underlying research may not have happened in the way it did or even at all without the support of a large number of people. I am most grateful to Edward Roderick, the enlightened chief executive of Christian Salvesen PLC who possibly had more confidence in my research methods and results than I did myself at times and afforded me the invaluable opportunity to work with more than 100 senior managers across the group over a period of more than seven years.

I am grateful to Fay Franscella who taught me the fundamentals of using the repertory grid technique, and introduced me to the work of George Kelly, and to Ann Huff and Colin Eden for their support on cognitive mapping, not a technique that many accountants had hitherto used. Many academics view action research as too close to business consultancy for comfort and fail to see the knowledge creation potential that may be derived from working so closely with organizational members, though with research councils emphasizing employer engagement and user strategies for research, this is changing. My thanks go to my academic colleagues who gave their support, especially the MCA members named in the preface and many more who participated in workshops and conferences.

My thanks also go to my colleague David Crowther at Leicester Business School for stimulating research in the department and for introducing me to Jonathan Norman at Gower, who together with series editor Darren Dalcher, encouraged me to write the book without any pressure, and have provided thoughtful and valuable feedback throughout.

Not many academics give public thanks to their Deans, often seen as people who attempt to control and give them too much work for them to find time for their research. Mine certainly keeps me busy, but is one of the kindest hearted and reasonable line managers as well as one of the best researchers in his field that I have had the privilege to work with, so a big thank you to David Wilson for his support.

Last but certainly not least, a big thank you to my husband Frank Cattley, who is both my greatest critic and best friend and has diligently proof-read virtually everything of any importance I have ever written, including my doctoral thesis and this book, though if there are any mistakes I of course take full responsibility.

PREFACE

Having worked with business clients in accountancy practice, my knowledge of the reality of business decision-making did correspond well with the rational economic models I studied to pass my professional accountancy examinations. This caused a tension when I started to teach financial management for professional accountancy students in 1985, and I found myself drawing more from the strategy literature I was exposed to as an MBA student at Kingston Business School to provide the context for project appraisal in my teaching.

As my academic career developed I became more involved in the design and delivery of management development programmes and more intrigued by the psychological explanations for management behaviour, which provided the motivation for my doctoral research. It was some time before I was fortunate enough to meet Roger Mills at Henley Management College, a Professor of Accounting and Finance who shared my dissatisfaction with the economics-based accounting literature and worked closely with practitioners who shared the same sense of reality of business decisions and project appraisal. Under his supervision I was encouraged to plan and execute an action research study that was at that time deemed so high risk (nowhere near as acceptable a methodology as it has become) that my proposal was subjected to a viva voce examination, a process usually reserved for the final thesis. The then external examiner Professor Tony Berry, having given me a hard time in the examination, later became a friend and introduced me to the Management Control Association (MCA), a network of researchers interested in the broad area of control and control processes in organizations. It was in this network that I presented much of my early work and I am grateful for the valuable debate it simulated and comments from Professors David Otley, Jane Broadbent, Tony Lowe and others who helped me to develop my ideas.

The underlying research and development of ideas for this book therefore started more than 10 years ago, at a time when risk registers and risk management were hardly spoken about, let alone as part of the commonplace day-to-day business discourse they are today. The first academic paper I had published on project risk assessment in 1999 is arguably more relevant now than it was then. Other research over the last 10 years has involved several co-authors and explored a number of related themes, not least the work with Professor Clive Emmanuel on managerial judgement in strategic investment decisions funded by CIMA. However, it has only been since I started teaching Project Management on the MBA at De Montfort University that my interest has developed more towards the implementation and risk management of projects. This prompted a review of research data on strategies for managing project risk, which combined with the critical comments on my papers from the project management community via the PMI and the APM, resulted in the structure for this book.

Whilst my principal job at the University is a management role, both as Head of Department managing staff and subject quality in Accounting and Finance, and as Head of the Graduate Centre managing the portfolio and delivery of postgraduate programmes, which leaves little time for my own research and teaching, intellectual curiosity is kept alive by working with PhD students. I have supervised or examined over 20 doctoral students, but the two who I have published with, Robin Woolley from South Africa and Samuel Komakech from Uganda have stretched my thinking the most in relation to project risk and decision-making. They have experienced a little of both the pain and the joy, working with me and engaging with practitioners on some of the research questions addressed in this book.

Elaine Pamela Harris

INTRODUCTION

RATIONALE FOR THE BOOK

Success in business comes down to two broad management skills, often termed as 'doing the right thing' (choosing the right projects) and 'doing things right' (good project management). First this book examines the challenges that managers face in assessing the likely risks and benefits that need to be taken into account when choosing projects. Then it explores the strategic level risks that will need to be dealt with in managing those projects and suggests risk management strategies. Often this link between strategic level appraisal of project opportunities and project risk management is not made. Evidence is taken from a number of research studies, including a longitudinal case study (in a single group of companies over an eight-year period), which suggests that this link is important.

All decisions about which projects an organization should choose are taken without certain knowledge of what the future will hold and how successful the project will be. Whilst decisions are taken in conditions of *uncertainty*, we can attempt to predict the factors that can impact on a project. Once we can identify these factors and their possible impacts we can call them *risks* and attempt to analyze and respond to them. Risks can be both positive, such as embedded opportunities, perhaps to do more business with a new client or customer in future. However, most people think of risks as negative, things that can go wrong, and those indeed require more focus in most risk management processes. This book deals with both the negative or downside risk and the positive or upside risk.

AIMS OF THE BOOK

The main aim of this book is to consider the strategic level risks that organizations may face when taking on projects of different types. A project is usually defined as such for project management purposes because it has a unique identity and a finite life and is thus distinguishable from other continuing operations. However, many projects have similar characteristics that are common to a number of projects experienced by the same or other organizations. This book aims to show how the use of a project typology can guide project risk management by identifying common risks shared by projects of each type. A framework is offered for analyzing strategic level project risks and case illustrations are provided to demonstrate the application of this framework for seven types of projects most often experienced in organizations today.

The aims of the book can be summarized as helping managers to:

- understand the strategic context for project risk management;
- appreciate a range of qualitative methods that can be used in project risk identification and analysis;
- identify and assess the strategic level risks attached to a specific project;
- develop appropriate risk management strategies for a specific project;
- consider the links between strategic analysis and project risk management;
- improve their project risk management skills;
- learn from project reviews.

STRUCTURE OF THE BOOK

The first part of the book, Chapters 1 and 2, sets the scene for strategic project risk appraisal. After setting out the rationale and aims of the book in the Introduction, the practical problems of project appraisal are explored in Chapter 1. The context is defined in terms of the project appraisal process and decision-making behaviour, drawing upon relevant literature and recent research findings. The common approaches to project risk management are considered before setting out the project typology used for the case illustrations in Chapters 3 to 9.

Chapter 2 discusses the qualitative methods that can be used both by practitioners and academics or consultants as a method of risk identification, in the co-creation of project relevant knowledge (action research). Qualitative methods drawn from cognitive psychology are first introduced in Chapter 2, which then explains how these methods can help managers to identify the risks that may impact on projects at the strategic investment decision stage. Chapter 2 has been kept purposefully short and relatively jargon free, so as to focus the book on the practical application of these techniques to a range of different types of project. The academic references provided may be followed up for a more detailed discussion of methods.

The main body of the book in Part 2 contains a chapter on each of seven types of strategic level project, setting out the definition and common characteristics of each type. Case examples are used to present risk attributes and risk management strategies for each type, using methods outlined in Chapter 2. These include visual maps of the most common sources of risk found in project risk research undertaken by the author and academic colleagues.

The third part of the book examines the issue of controllability in Chapter 10 and explores how the learning from early stage project risk appraisal (pre-decision) can benefit project management (post-decision), with practical implications for knowledge transfer from strategic decision-making to project management. Chapter 11 draws conclusions for project reviews. This supports the main argument of the book, that the early stage use of qualitative risk assessment methods can enhance the subsequent risk management of projects.

LIMITATIONS OF THE BOOK

As with other titles in this series, this book assumes a basic level of knowledge and understanding of the principles of project management, such as is found in the practitioner guides (PMI, 2008; APM, 2006).

The focus of this more specialist book is on qualitative methods in project risk appraisal. There are plenty of other books that deal with quantitative approaches, especially those written from a technical engineering perspective. This book is written from a Business School perspective and deals more with the human and organizational aspects often neglected in other texts. However, the two approaches are not mutually exclusive and project managers should develop their knowledge of both, at least to a sufficient level to be able to decide when and how to apply particular techniques.

PART 1
BACKGROUND TO PROJECT RISK APPRAISAL

CHAPTER 1

CONTEXT FOR STRATEGIC PROJECT RISK APPRAISAL

Project risk appraisal should begin before the organization makes its decision about whether to undertake a project or if faced with several options, which alternative to choose. This chapter sets the scene for pre-decision project risk assessment, when there is more uncertainty than measurable risk. Timing is important here, so the first section of this chapter deals with the project appraisal process, identifying stages in a project's development prior to the decision to commit to the project. This is before project management is assumed to begin.

Further sections explore the context in terms of decision-making behaviour and traditional approaches to project risk management. The last section develops the project typology that will be used in Part 2 to analyze the likely sources of risk affecting different types of project.

BACKGROUND TO THE PROJECT APPRAISAL PROCESS

In early accounting literature, rooted in economics, project appraisal was seen as part of capital budgeting, defined as 'the allocation of scarce resources between alternative uses so as to best obtain objectives ... over time' (Bromwich, 1976). This covered decisions on the total amount of capital expenditure a firm should undertake and the financing of projects as well as the decisions about which specific investment projects to accept. The main methods of project appraisal recommended, internal rate of return and net present value, were based on discounted cash flow (DCF) techniques.

The term capital budgeting also implied that capital expenditure decisions might be routinized into the overall budgeting process, usually within an annual planning cycle. In the case of investment in assets such as manufacturing equipment in established firms, where life cycles and capacity requirements may have been relatively predictable, this assumption may have been reasonable. However, with the more rapid change and complexity involved in advanced technology and the emergence of new knowledge-based industries, a fundamental change in our thinking about investment in projects has become necessary.

A view that DCF techniques misplaced the emphasis of capital budgeting was expressed (King, 1975) and a broader view advocated with multiple steps in the decision-making process, from triggering, screening and definition to evaluation, transmission and decision. However, it took time for this view to become widely accepted. The need to focus business planning more externally on the competitive environment and the shortening of time available to identify and evaluate new opportunities is well documented in the strategy literature, where investment decisions are more about the formulation and implementation of strategy. Recent research is concerned with strategic alignment of projects (Langfield-Smith, 2005).

Strategic investment decisions are still concerned with choosing 'between alternative(s) ... so as to best obtain objectives' (Bromwich, 1976), but involve a far broader consideration than the economics of the prospective project. Research in the 1980s and 1990s 'focused on the fit between the use of DCF techniques for capital expenditure evaluation and specific contingencies of business strategy, external environment, information systems characteristics, reward systems structure, and degree of decentralization' (Langfield-Smith, 2005).

Strategic investment decisions (SID) are required to deliver a business strategy and allow an organization to meet its business and financial goals. The SID process starts with the identification of a project opportunity or a number of alternative opportunities that compete for the allocation of organizational resources (money, people and capital equipment).

There are two broad schools of thought on the funding of projects. One is that capital is limited so there is a competition amongst business units and projects for it, named capital rationing. This may be true in times of economic downturn, especially when there is less inter-bank lending activity. The second school of thought is that if a potential project is good enough, especially if it is likely to generate exceptional profits, that capital can always be raised to fund it. The experience of most managers is that the reality in their organizations lies somewhere in between. There is usually some sort of capital constraint and thus an element of competition for funds. The SID process is all about defining a project opportunity and working up a business case to present to the funding providers, either internally to a group board, or externally to investors, or both.

Figure 1.1 shows a typical SID process for business development-type projects in a large divisionalized company in the logistics industry, where each business unit is responsible for scanning the environment for potential projects, often in the form of invitations to tender (ITT) for new business or contract renewal. This process model was supported as more generally relevant in a recent survey (Emmanuel, Harris and Komakech, 2009) with two additional post-decision steps identified of project implementation and change management to extend the model.

These further stages are most relevant to project managers, fitting between the final decision point (stage 6) and the project review (stage 7).

However, what is generally the case in most organizations is that the managers involved are different at the different stages. At stages 1 and 2 the business development managers or marketers are most involved. At the evaluation stage (stage 4) the management accountants or financial managers are most involved. A range of experts may be consulted at stages 2 (technical) and 3 (stakeholders) and the full divisional board may be involved at stage 5, but often project managers do not become involved until the decision has been taken at stage 6 and responsibility is allocated to a project manager to form a team to implement the project. Thus the evaluation of risks and returns has already taken place. (How) is this knowledge transferred? Does the project manager see a copy of any early stage project risk assessment?

We will return to these questions in Chapter 10.

It is important to note here that whilst the model in Figure 1.1 is generally found to operate in a similar way in many organizations, not just in the logistics industry, the ideas for project opportunities can emanate from different parts of the organization. If the opportunity is to take over another business it may come from the firm's bank or financial advisers or from a direct approach from the vendor at top management level. Likewise, the project may be formulated to comply with new legislation, so may emanate from the firm's lawyers or if employment law, from the human resources department. The differences in the above model that may be found for projects of specific types are considered further in Part 2 of this book. For any type of project the potential involvement of multiple managers in the process brings decision-making behaviour and psychology in particular, into consideration.

DECISION-MAKING BEHAVIOUR

Simon (1947) was one of the earliest and most acclaimed researchers to write about the psychology of organizational decisions. He identified the problems of assuming economic rationality in a process reliant on human behaviour, and of the roles of authority and communication. Later editions added sections on information processing, organizational design and the selective perception of executives (Simon, 1976). However, many lessons from this work seem to have been neglected. This book aims to put such issues firmly back on the management agenda, as it is argued that they are even more relevant in the context of project management, governance and accountability in today's corporate world.

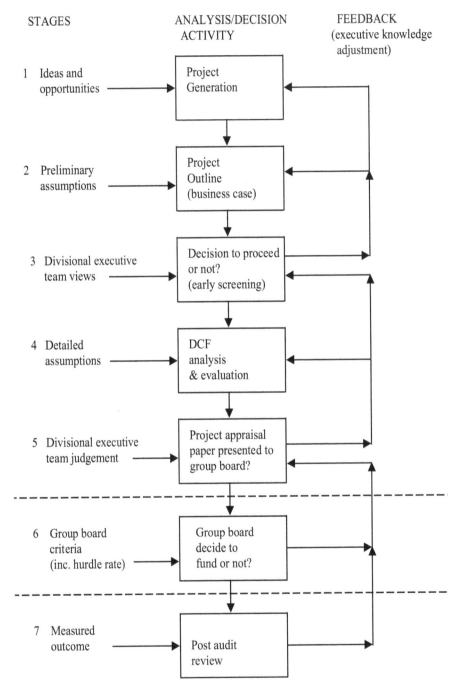

Figure 1.1   Strategic investment appraisal process
Source: Harris (1999)

Kahneman and Tversky (1979) developed prospect theory, which also contradicted the economic rational model of decision-making. They found that people do not use probabilistic calculations to ascertain the economically optimal solutions, but that they exaggerate downside risks if they are risk averse and may exaggerate the chances of success when faced with upside risks, for example by buying a lottery ticket at low cost with little chance of a potentially high gain. This kind of behaviour is just one of the 'heuristics' found in the psychology of decision-making.

Tversky and Kahneman (1981) also found that people react differently to the same prospect if it is presented differently, known as the framing effect. Framing experiments focus on how the gains and losses of an option are presented from a zero or other reference point to give the decision-maker a different impression of the same set of cash flows. This work on the psychology of intuitive judgement has been extended to include many examples of heuristics and types of bias in decision-making (Gilovich, Griffin and Kahneman, 2002).

One of the newer examples is the 'affect' heuristic, which deals with the emotive or intuitive response to certain words or phrases used in describing or framing a prospect (Slovic et al., 2002). It extends the framing concept to include the language used to define a project in addition to the presentation of financial data. When decision-makers assess the risks of a project opportunity they may respond differently to the same prospect if colourful or emotive language is used.

It may be recognized that such language is used to advantage in marketing consumer products, but this affect heuristic could also be used by project champions to elicit a positive response when trying to sell their ideas to executives to gain approval for projects or by others in the organization wishing to create a negative response, for example to avoid organizational change.

Bazerman (2006) has worked on the area of managerial judgement in decision-making from an organizational behaviour perspective for over 25 years, adding to and editing chapters from the first edition published in 1985. The focus of the work is on helping individuals overcome personal bias in order to make better managerial decisions. Hastie and Dawes (2001) also examine the role of personal bias in decision-making and the conflict between mathematically-based decision methods using probability theory and human information processing. They examine the psychology of judgement in investment decisions, but they tend to focus on individuals making stock market investments rather than business managers evaluating strategic project opportunities.

Whilst much of this work has been updated to place more emphasis on investment decisions, the problem is that it is still largely focused at the level of the individual, thus neglecting the strategic context of groups of managers acting together in decision-making processes in large organizations. The affect heuristic was found to influence managers in the mining industry in their perceptions of the risks and benefits of an activity (Dunbar, 2007). The focus on the individual is acknowledged by Dunbar, who suggests future research on framing effects might explore how this affects decision-making within groups. Simon (1947) recognized the role that organizational structure and culture have in creating the decision-making environment for managers.

Bower (1986, first published in 1972) first examined the group process, which he named the 'impetus' stage in decision-making, to describe the rate of progress of the proposal upward through the organizational hierarchy. Mintzberg et al. (1976) also identified the importance of internal politics and persuasion to gain consensus. Neither study examined the psychological phenomena of framing or heuristics explicitly in their research, coming from a more sociological perspective.

Helliar et al. (2001) tested the framing effect by designing alternative scenarios in a questionnaire used to explore UK managers' attitudes to risk in decision situations. They found that 'the framing of a decision in terms of gains or losses was critical in determining whether a manager would adopt a risk-seeking or risk-avoiding stance' (Helliar et al., 2001, p. 87). They grouped the risks perceived by the managers they interviewed into four categories: financial, labour-related, strategic and miscellaneous. The strategic risks 'ranged from concern about market share to fear of being taken over' (Helliar et al., 2001, p. 85). This type of risk might be expected to be more emotive and therefore more subject to the affect heuristic than, say, financial risks, where variability of returns or trade credit risks could be quantified, though this was not specifically tested.

PROJECT RISK MANAGEMENT

Collier, Berry and Burke (2007) used exploratory cases and a survey to investigate risk management practices in UK companies. Whilst there was no particular focus on strategic investment decisions or project risk assessment, there were interesting findings on managers' attitudes to risk. They found that 'heuristic methods of risk management were used much more than the systems-based approach that is associated with risk management in much of the literature, at least at the corporate level' and 'the methods in highest use were the more subjective ones (particularly experience) ... reinforcing the role of the human actor over analytical techniques' (Collier, Berry and Burke, 2007, p. 117). They also found that organizational stance towards risk was important in determining risk management practices.

The approach to project risk management taken in the project management literature (PMI, 2008) is a six-phase risk management process, from planning and identification through qualitative and quantitative risk analysis to risk response planning, and monitoring and control. The key technique for assessing the risks associated with a project is to estimate the probability of a specific source of risk affecting the project and assess the impact such effect might have.

This can be done mathematically, using probability theory, or subjectively using qualitative methods. Chapman and Ward (2003) devote a whole chapter to estimation as probability theory is not widely understood by business managers. The probabilities may be represented in a probability impact grid (PIG), which seeks to quantify the effect of risks on project outcomes (see for example, Webb, 2003, p. 124). This formed the basis of early risk management software such as RISKMAN (Carter et al., 1994) and was expressed as:

$$Risk\ exposure = impact\ value \times probability\ of\ occurrence$$

The model is simple, but the data inputs to the model still rely on subjective judgement. It has been shown that when people are asked to estimate the frequency or chance of a risk or hazard occurring (perceived risk), they tend to overestimate low probabilities (compared to technical estimates based on known frequencies) and underestimate high probabilities (Slovic, 2000, p. 116). This can also apply to the impact or consequences, where people tend to overestimate the impact of high consequence events. When combined in a low probability high consequence event, the risk exposure will be magnified. Recognizing the psychological limitations of subjective estimation and the instability of estimation over time (as people react to new information) is important in risk assessment and project management. The danger of turning the risk exposure into a number by multiplying two estimates together is that it gives the analysis a more scientific appearance than is really the case, implying a level of *accuracy* that may be misleading.

The other limitation in the application of this type of risk assessment is the *completeness* of analysis, as not all relevant sources of risk may have been identified. When projects fail it can be due to a risk that no one perceived when the project was evaluated. For this reason there are a number of approaches that might be taken at the risk identification stage to ensure all significant risk sources are captured, including checklists. These may be generic, as in the risk breakdown structure presented in PMBOK® (PMI, 2008, p. 280) or specific to a type of project, for example new product development (Webb, 2003, p. 42). Other approaches are outlined in a specialist APM guide (Hopkinson et al., 2008).

Risk assessment may be quantitative, using a risk model or simulation to estimate exposure, as described above, or it may be qualitative, 'describing characteristics of each risk in sufficient detail to allow them to be understood' (Hillson and Murray-Webster, 2005, p. 20). Qualitative methods have the advantage of surfacing issues of risk attitude and sharing of ideas between participants, helping to develop a common language for risk description in a business team or organization. Best practice risk identification can also harness the emotional literacy/intelligence of participants (Hillson and Murray-Webster, 2005, p. 112).

This book will show how such qualitative methods may be applied to a range of different project types (categories of projects that share common characteristics). The typology used is developed next.

PROJECT TYPOLOGY

More and more organizations are using project management to separate out activities that can benefit from a structured approach and calling them projects. In addition to more conventional projects such as the purchase or construction of new buildings or facilities, changes in business processes and automation of production or services are also defined as projects. Whilst computerization of administrative processes has led to many information technology (IT) projects being identified, the management of transition or change may also be defined in project terms. This is sometimes labelled 'projectification' and has led to the number and variety of projects requiring categorization in some way (Crawford, Hobbs and Turner, 2006), especially for risk management purposes.

In a recent research study, 91 CIMA members working in 65 companies participated in a survey, with responses across 24 industries. Table 1.1 shows the types of projects the respondents had experience of. There were seven categories, including 'other' that over 30 per cent of these managers had some involvement with. They then chose a single project in one of the categories to focus their thoughts on for the rest of the survey.

Many respondents had a financial background, which perhaps explains why 60 per cent had involvement in business acquisitions and 70 per cent in new systems projects. The percentages might well vary for other managers with more mixed backgrounds. There was high variation within the 'other' category, so excluding this there are six main project types which are explored in this book, though taken in a different sequence. They are all project types the author has experienced as a researcher or as a manager in higher education, or both. Each project type is defined in Part 2 in terms of the common characteristics before the risks are explored. A seventh category was added to this list due to the author's own experience of project managing events such as workshops and conferences, to share the personal learning from these events.

Table 1.1   Project types

	Experienced		Focus
Type of project in your SID experience	Count	%	%
New technology or infrastructure, e.g. computer systems projects	64	70	18
New site or site development (new location, relocation, expansion)	62	68	21
Acquisitions of business assets or companies	55	60	26
New product development	43	47	14
Other, e.g. decommissioning, downsizing, business process design	42	46	9
New market development (new customers/clients)	38	42	11
Compliance (new legislation, e.g. health and safety)	31	34	1
Total			100

Source: Emmanuel, Harris and Komakech, 2009

The new market development (new customer) projects listed sixth in Table 1.1 above are analyzed first in Part 2 as they were the most common project type observed in the longitudinal study that forms the main evidence base for this book. It is also this type of project which was primarily used to develop the methods set out in the next chapter.

CHAPTER 2

PROJECT RISK APPRAISAL TECHNIQUES

This chapter sets out a project risk appraisal framework drawn from cognitive psychology developed by the author in an action research project. It sets out the qualitative methods that can be used both as research methods to discover how a person makes sense of a topic, and as a means for managers to identify sources of risk in relation to strategic investment opportunities. They are drawn from cognitive psychology and are all based on a theory of cognition. Personal construct theory (PCT) developed by Kelly (1955) is a theory of cognition that suggests that people make sense of their world by sorting each new experience into a set of bipolar constructs (opposite concepts) by reference to previous experience.

To assess the attractiveness of a new project opportunity an organizational member will recall features of previous projects; both approved and rejected, successes and failures. In order to differentiate one project from another, sufficient information is needed to compare and contrast prospective projects on a number of features or characteristics. To assess the riskiness of the alternatives, the projects may be compared using a series of concepts that contribute to the overall level of risk. These may be regarded as project risk attributes or risk drivers. One such concept might be the level of novelty, such that a new project which is very similar to previous ones might be regarded as low novelty and therefore low risk. In contrast a research and development project involving technical innovation and a new target market might have a high level of novelty and therefore a high risk attached.

Three methods of eliciting personal constructs that may be used separately or combined in project risk identification are the nominal group technique (NGT), a form of brainstorming designed for use with groups; repertory grid technique; and cognitive mapping. For these methods to be applied in an attempt to identify group cognition or a shared understanding of a topic, in this case project risk, there should be a preliminary test to establish if Kelly's commonality and sociality corollaries apply (Kelly, 1955).

In the context of managers in an organization, this means ascertaining if they have sufficient common ground to reach shared views of project opportunities. Commonality means the individual managers will have shared or common understandings, thinking about the risk drivers in a similar way. Sociality means that whilst the members of the group may not always agree or hold a shared view, they can understand and appreciate the views expressed by others in the group and find ways to reach agreement even where there is not absolute consensus. Where organizational members have worked together in the same organization for some time (such that they have shared experiences of previous projects they have evaluated and undertaken) these corollaries are likely to hold when they discuss new projects, even if their attitudes to risk differ. Working together in an established management team and having gained experience of working in the same industrial sector will auger well for reaching a shared understanding of project risk.

Ask the same people to give their views on topics such as politics or religion, where non-work experiences will have shaped their thinking and one might expect considerable variation of views and difficulty reaching anything close to consensus. For this reason, these methods are less appropriate for use with newly formed groups or with surrogates such as student groups. The facilitator will need to assess the group profile and observe the team dynamics in order to ensure that the commonality and sociality assumptions are reasonable.

RISK IDENTIFICATION TECHNIQUES

Nominal Group Technique

The first of the three methods, the nominal group technique (NGT) relies less on Kelly's underlying PCT principles, but where the aim is to elicit a group view, then commonality and sociality will help the process. NGT is a two-stage process where a facilitator sets out the topic or focus of discussion and first tasks each individual to brainstorm a topic in silence and note down their thoughts (Delbecq et al., 1975). The second stage involves the group members sharing and developing their thoughts through a facilitated discussion, rather like a focus group. Results may be captured by a facilitator using a flip chart. It is this group process element of the technique that differentiates it from the more widely known Delphi technique, which usually canvasses opinion from individuals. Any aggregation or summarizing tends to be undertaken by the facilitator or interviewer rather than through a group discussion. For project risk identification and analysis, there is high value in the group discussion and shared sense making part of the process.

The aim is to encourage all members to contribute and discourage any dominant group members from unduly influencing others. In other words, agreement with someone else's view should not occur simply due to the identity and position in the organization of the individual, but may occur through negotiation and discussion based on an evaluation of the arguments or rationale. The result of the facilitated discussion should be to reach agreed conclusions. In the context of project risk the conclusions may be on the drivers of risk for a project opportunity and on the perceived level of risk attached, though this may require more than one discussion, especially where the technique is also new.

This technique can be used simply for risk identification, prior to risk analysis, or it may be used right through risk analysis to risk response and fed directly into the project risk register.

Repertory Grid Technique

The repertory grid technique (RGT) is a grid drawn up with instances of a phenomenon in the participants' range of experience as the columns (elements) and the attributes (constructs) used to differentiate the elements as rows (see Table 2.1). It is usual for the participants to select the elements as representative, in this case of projects within their experience, and to generate the constructs by a process of comparison of three elements (triads) at a time (Cassell and Walsh, 2004). Participants start with a focus of investigation, in this case project risk, and are asked to say what makes two out of three elements the same (marked S in Table 2.1) and the third one different (D) and give it a label. The extremes of the construct may also be labelled as the poles of a continuum that elements can be assessed against.

For example, if comparing three new product development projects within the participants' recall, one may stand out as having greater novelty than the other two, so the construct may be labelled 'novelty' with high and low novelty as the bipolar reference points. Other projects can then be assessed on a scale (say 1 to 5) from low to high novelty (see Repertory Grid Technique, pages 22–24).

RGT was first developed for use with individuals, and their scores may have been aggregated to make up a group assessment. RGT can be used with individuals

Table 2.1   Repertory grid example

Elements (acquisitions)	A	B	C	D
Constructs (project risk attributes)				
1. Strategic location	D	S	S	
2. Integration (with existing operations)	D	S		S
3. Familiarity with territory	D	S		S
4.	D	S		S
5.	D		S	S
6.		D	S	S

Source: Adapted from Harris, 2007, p1064

or with groups (Johnson and Johnson, 2002). It is important for groups to define each construct to ensure they have a shared understanding of the term. For use in a project risk assessment framework, where managers will have cause to refer to the project risk constructs when discussing later projects or during post audit reviews, it is advisable to capture these in a glossary of terms. Limitations of RGT in knowledge acquisition are discussed by Rugg and Shadbolt (1991).

One of the main benefits of using the RGT for project risk identification is that it can easily be used to prioritize the risks and to analyze the levels of risk from each source, thus putting risk scores into the grid, turning a qualitative method into a quantitative tool, as RGT was designed to do (Fransella and Bannister, 1977). This is illustrated in the section on Repertory Grid Technique, (pages 22–24) and presented for business development projects in Chapter 3.

Cognitive Mapping

Cognitive mapping uses a visual representation of constructs, organized around the central theme, rather like a mind map (Eden, 1988). It tends to reflect multiple levels or hierarchies of constructs, whereby detailed or subordinate constructs can be clustered or grouped into higher order constructs, elicited by a process of laddering (Rugg and McGeorge, 1995). Its use in generating strategic options and formulating strategy has developed (Eden and Simpson, 1989) over the last 20 years (Huff and Jenkins, 2002). Analysis of failed projects has produced useful insights into project risk (Williams et al., 2005), but to benefit organizations in terms of avoiding or mitigating risks it needs to be used in the risk identification process at the earliest possible pre-decision stage, especially in innovation projects where uncertainties are high (Harris and Woolley, 2009).

Cognitive mapping has advantages over the hierarchical risk breakdown structure (PMI, 2008, p. 280) as it can show inter-relationships between the risk attributes and is a more dynamic tool. To get the maximum benefit from this method, the definition of each construct should be recorded. If mapped manually using oval record cards, these can be written on the reverse of the card, with the construct label on the front. If specific mapping software or a PowerPoint presentation is used, these can be stored as notes.

Figure 2.1 shows the risk breakdown structure presented in PMBOK® redrawn as a basic cognitive map (PMI, 2008, p. 280). It can be seen that it would be easy to link factors across the clusters of project risks, for example technical requirements (linked by dotted line) with project management communication, thus making inter-relationships explicit. Limitations of cognitive mapping are discussed in Harris (2007) and Harris and Woolley (2009), the main one being the arguments about group or shared cognition as opposed to aggregation of individuals' cognition. The main advantage, however, is that the resulting map is based on managers'

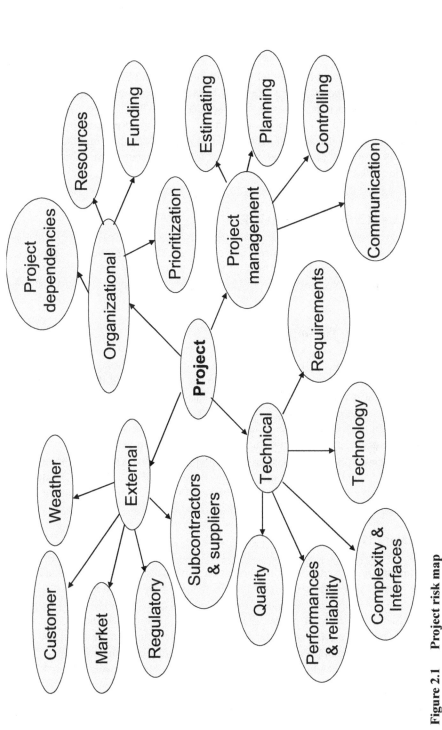

Figure 2.1   Project risk map

knowledge and experience, part of which is tacit or held in the subconscious, so only accessible by psychological methods.

Cognitive mapping can be used with or without RGT, and both RGT and cognitive mapping can be used with or without the NGT. All three methods have been used by the author at various stages in the cases set out in Part 2. The risks shown in the project risk map in Figure 2.1 are generic. The maps presented in Chapters 3 to 9 are specific to the seven different project types. Maps are most useful when derived by project appraisal teams and redrawn after group discussion by project management teams.

RISK ANALYSIS TECHNIQUES

Following the same three methods, set out in the section above, for identifying project risks, the risks can then be analyzed by prioritizing each risk area (for an individual project or category of projects) and assessing the level of risk using an agreed scale.

Nominal Group Technique

Following the identification of project risks through the brainstorming process described above, the next step might be to list the risks in order of importance, with the highest priority risk at the top of the list and the lowest priority at the bottom. This is akin to making a subjective judgement about the impact each sort of risk might have on a project. The level of risk attached to a specific project can then be assessed, by each individual and then the group assessing whether there is a high, medium or low risk of each risk impacting on the project. This may not appear to be a very scientific method, but at the earliest stages of consideration of a prospective project, it is often the best sort of project risk assessment that is cost-effective.

Repertory Grid Technique

The next section explains, with an illustration, how to use the project risks identified in the repertory grid earlier in this chapter by following these steps:

1. Identify sources of project risk agreed by the group (see above).
2. Assess the relative importance of each attribute (assign weightings).
3. Assess the risk profile of a project on each attribute (raw scores).
4. Apply the weightings from step 2 to calculate the weighted risk score (grid).
5. Interpret the score along with financial appraisal measures (matrix).

Step 1. Identify sources of project risk   The example used here is taken from research in a large logistics company, where 12 project risk attributes were found. The last two are not included here, as they are more specific to the logistics sector, and 10 is sufficient to illustrate the technique. Each attribute should ideally be broken down into several subcategories and discussed at length, but the aim is to establish a cost-effective decision-support technique which focuses managers' attention on key risk areas.

Step 2. Assess the relative importance of each attribute   If for a particular type of project the attributes found at step 1 are of unequal importance, e.g. expertise has a greater bearing on the project's risk profile than cultural fit, the next step is to agree appropriate weightings. This can be achieved in a number of ways. The simplest is to start with equal weightings and move values up or down from there. In the above example, with 10 project risk attributes, each would start at 10 per cent. Unless some are significantly reduced, say to 5 per cent and others significantly increased, say to 20 per cent, this step is not required, as it will not impact enough on the overall score calculated at step 4. See step 4 for illustration.

Step 3. Assess the risk profile of a project on each attribute   This can, of course, be undertaken by an individual such as the project proposer (who may best understand the issues) or by the accountant (based on all the 'business case' information available). This may be appropriate in smaller businesses. However, in larger organizations it should be carried out on a group basis, e.g. by the divisional management team, using a consensus seeking debating process.

Table 2.2   Project risk attributes example

---

1. Strategic fit (the risk of operating outside an agreed strategy).
2. Expertise (the risk of not having the right sort of expertise for the project).
3. Image (the potential damage to the company's reputation which may arise).
4. Size (the risk of putting 'too many eggs in one basket').
5. Complexity (the number and interdependence of assumptions involved).
6. Planning timescale (the time pressure to make a decision and to deliver).
7. Cultural fit (the potential for misunderstanding between parties to the project).
8. Quality of information (unreliable, insufficient or invalid assumptions).
9. Demands of customer (unreasonable expectations or requirements).
10. Environmental factors (impact of political, economic, social or technical factors).

Source: Adapted from Harris (1999)

A scoring system is used to assess the risk profile of the project, by scoring the project on a scale of say 1 to 5 for each attribute. In this case, 1 indicates low risk, 5 high risk, 3 average risk (in the company's experience), with 2 and 4 as intermediate points. These are recorded in a grid as raw scores (see step 4 for illustration).

Step 4. Calculate the weighted risk score   This step involves calculating a weighted average project risk score by applying the weightings from step 2 to the raw score from step 3. A simple average can be used if risk attributes are considered to be of roughly equal importance (see step 2 above).

The illustrative project is one with a good strategic fit, with a single existing customer, where there are generally good working relations, but the customer wants the company to deliver services to its new European subsidiary in a very short timescale. There is insufficient time available to properly validate efficiency assumptions before the deal must be agreed (to avoid a European competitor gaining the business).

Table 2.3 shows the results of step 3 in column 1, step 2 in column 2, and step 4 in column 3. The weighted risk score of 3 shows the project to be of average risk (on a

Table 2.3   Project risk assessment grid

	1	2	3
Attributes	**Assessment**	**Weighting**	**Weighted**
(sources of risk)	**(x raw score)**	**(w %)**	**(wx)**
1) Strategic fit	1	5	0.05
2) Expertise	2	10	0.20
3) Image	1	5	0.05
4) Size	3	15	0.45
5) Complexity	3	10	0.30
6) Planning timescale	5	15	0.75
7) Cultural fit	1	5	0.05
8) Quality of information	4	20	0.80
9) Demands of Customer	2	10	0.20
10) Environmental factors	3	5	0.15
Totals	25	100	3.00

scale of 1 to 5). Without the weightings from step 2 the overall score would have been 2.5 (25/10), which highlights the impact of weighting in this case. Whether a simple or weighted average is used, the effects of averaging can be dangerous if only the overall score is considered. It can be seen that the planning timescale (0.75) and the quality of information (0.80) are contributing over half (1.55) to the total of 3.00.

Step 5. Interpret the score along with financial appraisal measures   In combining the result from the project risk assessment grid from step 4 with the usual financial appraisal measures, e.g. NPV or internal rate of return (IRR), a useful decision support matrix can be constructed.

Table 2.4 shows an example of a project appraisal matrix. The hurdle points used on the vertical axis of the project appraisal matrix may be derived by ascertaining the cost of capital (in this case 12 per cent), and the target rate of return for risky projects, which is often higher, for a number of reasons (in this case 18 per cent). The hurdle points used on the horizontal axis of the matrix are a matter of managerial choice, but one might expect to have a fairly narrow marginal band around the midpoint, but not necessarily equally distributed (in this case a score of 2.5 to 3.3).

The project assessed above obtained a risk score of 3 which fits into the medium risk band. If the IRR calculated on the expected outcome or base case scenario (which may or may not incorporate probabilities) was 15 per cent, the case for the project to go ahead would be questionable (?). However, if the project return was calculated at 20 per cent, the case for the project could easily be made (✓). If the return fell below the cost of capital, at say 10 per cent, the case would be difficult to argue, unless loss of existing business from this customer was argued to be possible, but not reflected in the cash flow or calculated IRR.

Table 2.4   Project appraisal matrix

Project return (IRR)	Project risk Low (<2.5)	(weighted score) Med (2.5 – 3.3)	High (>3.3)
High (>18%)	✓	✓	?
Med (12–18%)	✓	?	X
Low (<12%)	?	X	X

As with any decision aid, the matrix does not give management the answer. There is still managerial judgement to be exercised, especially where any attribute is scored as 5 (high risk). However, it does provide guidance, which takes into account both the quantitative analysis from the DCF and the slightly more subjective assessment from the project risk assessment. It comes with the usual warning about not placing too much emphasis on a single measure (which of course applies to the IRR as well). This technique was registered by the author as *Pragmatix*®, which stands for Project Risk Assessment Grid and Matrix.

The project appraisal matrix is one use of the project risk assessment, as part of a strategic decision-making process, but there are further issues to consider in formulating a management response (see below).

Cognitive Mapping

The main use of the cognitive map is the iterative process necessary to produce a visual representation of a project that members of the group recognize as capturing the risk picture of a specific project or category of projects. It often needs to be redrawn several times to display all the inter-relationships between risk factors, which results from detailed discussions that help the group to articulate and develop their understanding of the risk profile of the project.

This discussion itself forms project risk analysis, with the final cognitive map displaying the agreed result. The ovals in the map can then be colour-coded to indicate the likely importance of the risks, either using traffic light colours, where red would be high risk, amber medium risk and green low or upside risk. This has been applied to the risks in Figure 2.1 using the author's priorities as a possible assessment for illustrative purposes (see Figure 2.2).

Figure 2.2 shows six risk areas assessed as high risk shaded red (darkest shading), which may be interconnected. In the technical area, the complexity and interfaces may have high levels of uncertainty which relate to the specification of requirements and externally to the number of subcontractors and suppliers. This in turn makes estimating and communications difficult in the project management area, which may impact on the availability of funding if the group board considers the risk too high for the likely returns. The solid line arrows show the main hierarchical relationships between the constructs and the dotted line arrows suggest the inter-relationships between constructs. There can be rather a lot of these which can confuse the picture, so whilst they are often used in cognitive mapping research (see Edkins et al., 2007), they are only used sparingly throughout this book. The reason for using them in Figure 2.2 is to illustrate the added potential that cognitive maps have over risk breakdown structure diagrams to show a more dynamic picture of the risks.

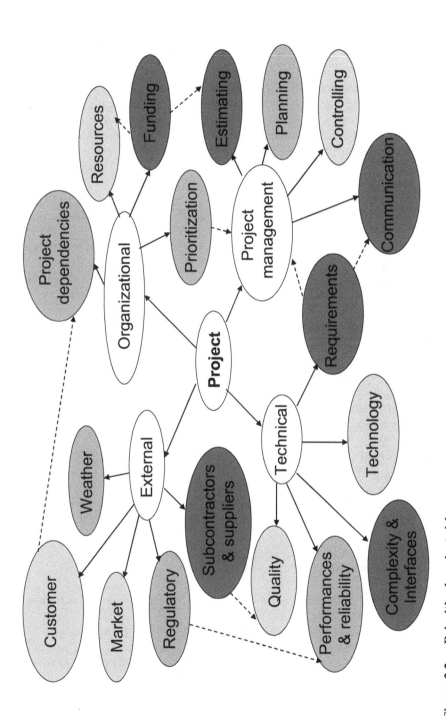

Figure 2.2   Prioritized project risk map

There are six risk areas assessed as low risk shaded green (lightest shading), and the remaining six assessed as medium risk shaded amber (medium shading) to complete the colour coding. The ovals labelled external, technical, organizational and project management are cluster names, so are not colour-coded in this example. The colour coding helps managers to prioritize which areas require the most attention when considering their response. This is covered in the section below. The risk map does not replace the risk register as a record of risks identified for specific projects, but is a helpful form for displaying risks at the planning stage before recording and prioritizing risks in the form of a register at the control stage.

MANAGEMENT RESPONSE TO PROJECT RISK APPRAISAL

The project risk assessment techniques outlined above may be used at different points in a project's life to aid management planning, decision-making and control. The amount of time which may elapse between a project opportunity first being identified and its formal board approval may be measured in days, months or even years (see Chapter 1).

Smaller decisions may be made more quickly, and may not require a full proposal document with detailed DCF analysis, but may benefit from the application of steps 1 and 3, using the attributes identified at step 1 as a checklist for assessment at step 3, and some consideration of response to the risk profile (step 6). Larger projects may benefit from the early application of steps 1 to 3, to screen out projects which are too risky to warrant further analysis.

Larger projects can benefit from re-assessment at a post audit stage, to learn how the risks have changed over the early period of implementation, and contribute to project management and control. This form of risk assessment really comes into its own, when it is tracked over time. By identifying the sources of risk, it is possible to take management action in response to a project risk score, before the outcome of the project is known.

Responses to 'marginal' risk scores may include:

- accept the risk and keep a close watch on the highest contributing attributes;
- pass on an element of the risk to the customer, e.g. by contract terms;
- charge a premium price which increases the return (into 'high' category);
- reformulate the project to do it differently in some way, such that risk is reduced.

Responses to a 'high' risk score may include:

- any or all of the above;
- delay the decision if possible until better information can be obtained or a major reformulation of the project can be considered;
- reduce the scale of the project or disaggregate it into separate phases with multiple decision points (known as real options approach);
- cover or insure some aspect of the risk via a third party;
- reject or abandon the project.

Most businesses could benefit from using this form of project risk assessment at some stage in their development. Potential benefits include:

- extra confidence in decisions made;
- less time spent on planning 'reject' proposals;
- extra efficiency in resource allocation;
- identification of key factors for project management and control;
- organizational learning by sharing managerial perceptions of project risk;
- enhancing managerial judgement exercised in decision-making.

RGT may take some time and resource to set up. In larger firms it may be necessary to call upon a consultant to help with these steps, especially to facilitate group-based assessment when step 3 in the repertory grid technique is first used. A trial could be undertaken using surrogate attributes in the first instance to test out the process before investing in development of the technique. Step 4 can easily be built into a spreadsheet model.

Steps 3, 5 and 6 may be open to as much manipulation and behavioural problems as other forms of project appraisal, where post hoc rationalization for projects is made after managers have become psychologically attached to projects. However, these potential problems can be overcome, by means of internal audit, or by developing links with reward systems, and by encouraging a culture where some risk taking is viewed positively as long as it is carefully assessed.

PART 2
STRATEGIC PROJECT RISK CASE ILLUSTRATIONS

CHAPTER 3

BUSINESS DEVELOPMENT PROJECTS

DEFINITION

Business development projects (BDP) may be a term used in business to business marketing, also known as new customer projects, market development or external client type projects. They involve securing a new customer for existing products or services, usually with a new contract, or contract renewal with an existing customer where the customer is likely to consider their options to take their business elsewhere. This type of project is contrasted with a new product development (NPD) which is dealt with in Chapter 6. A certain amount of tailoring the product or service to meet customer requirements may be involved, but it is largely a tried and tested product or service delivered to a new customer or anew to an existing customer whose contract has or may be about to expire.

CHARACTERISTICS

Many BDPs start with an invitation to tender (ITT) whereby the customer identifies a need, outlines their requirements and selects a supplier. They may also be initiated by the supplier advertising their products or services, for instance in the trade press and also apply to retail environments, for example financial services. Usually some sort of contract is signed, though this can be predetermined using a standard form rather than bespoke.

These projects are characterized as customer facing, where an external client or customer is in the driving seat, specifying their requirements. The first problem that may arise is where the customer does not fully understand the specification of products or services available, or their own customer needs. This can cause significant uncertainty at the outset, with project definition problems emanating from the customer. Prior to securing such a contract there will be a discovery and educational process required.

Prior to securing the business and a signed contract, there will be a competitive scenario where the result of clarification of customer requirements may lead the customer to cancel or shift their interest to a competitor. Time is usually of the essence, and short deadlines for submitting a tender or proposal put pressure on the project appraisal team. The window of opportunity may be short and delaying the contract while better information is gathered may be a limited option.

In this context, the business proposal will be put together quickly and only limited time spent on risk identification and analysis. This is why it is advisable for organizations that experience this type of project on a frequent basis to spend time building up a knowledge base and using a predetermined set of risks for BDP-type projects in assessing the level of risk of each such opportunity.

BDP RISK ATTRIBUTES

The 13 project risk attributes shown in four clusters in Table 3.1 were found in the main case study in a large logistics business for BDP projects, using a combination of the nominal group technique and the repertory grid technique (see Chapter 2).

Table 3.1   Project risk attributes for business development projects

Project Risk Attributes	Brief definition (see full glossary in appendix)
CORPORATE FACTORS: Strategic fit Expertise Impact	Potential contribution to strategy Level of expertise available compared to need Potential impact on company/brand reputation
PROJECT OPPORTUNITY: Size Complexity Planning timescale Quality of customer/supplier	Scale of investment, time and volume of work Number of and association between assumptions Time available to develop proposal pre-decision Credit checking, etc. added during version 4 updates
EXTERNAL FACTORS: Cultural fit Quality of information Demands of customer(s) Environmental	Matching set of values, beliefs and practices of parties Reliability, validity and sufficiency of base data Challenge posed by specific customer requirements Likely impact of PEST factors, inc. TUPE*
COMPETITIVE POSITION: Market strength Proposed contract terms	Power position of company in contract negotiations Likely contract terms and possible risk transference

* TUPE stands for the Transfer of Undertakings (Protection of Employment) regulations established in the UK in 1981 and revised in 2006. For further information see www.berr. gov.uk/employment/trade.../tupe/page16289.html

Source: Adapted from Harris, 1999

During the development (action research) phase there was a lot of discussion about whether strategic fit was really a risk or whether it was more of a prerequisite for the project to be considered at all. It was decided by participants that it was both and hence it remains. Interestingly, strategic alignment is identified as an under-researched aspect of capital budgeting (Langfield-Smith, 2005). It is also an example of a risk factor which can be regarded as either positive or negative when assessing a proposal. Many other attributes included in Table 3.1 can be assessed as upside or downside risk, including expertise, impact, cultural fit, market strength. This shows that risks were not just seen as hazards or problems in this organization, but also as opportunities, which was quite forward thinking at the time.

The fourth risk attribute in the project opportunity cluster, the quality of customer/supplier was added after a review meeting where the group finance director suggested that financial risks were perhaps not adequately covered. There were two areas of concern. One was the risk that a contracting party went out of business before they had fulfilled their contract obligations. There was a credit check undertaken as part of due diligence before contracts were actually signed, but it was felt that those organizational members, for example business development managers, who had face-to-face contact with customers, would be best placed to assess this risk at the early pre-decision stage. Feedback from others indicated this was reasonable, so the company's user guide for project risk assessment was updated to include this extra attribute.

The second area related to asset specificity of the fixed assets invested in for the project, as many were so client-specific that resale or re-use values built into the DCF analysis could be at high risk. It was suggested by others in the meeting that this aspect of risk could be built into the sensitivity analysis in the DCF presented in the project paper, and that it may also be considered within the existing risk attributes of complexity and quality of information, which relate to the planning assumptions.

BDP RISK ASSESSMENT

The example shown in Table 3.2 is the result of an assessment exercise facilitated by the researcher. It was assessed as higher than average risk overall (3.59 on a scale of 1 to 5). The risk scoring system is based around 3 being the normal level of risk attached to projects of this type in the assessor's experience, 2 is low risk and 1 is very low risk (or upside risk), 4 is high risk and 5 is very high risk (downside risk). This project, with an overall score of 3.59 is therefore assessed as above average risk for projects of its type. However, more important than the overall score is which risk attributes are contributing the most to that score, in other words the highest risk factors.

Table 3.2   BDP project risk assessment grid showing weighted score

RISK ATTRIBUTES	ASSESSMENT Raw Score x	WEIGHTING Weight w	WEIGHTED Score wx
Corporate factors:			
Strategic fit	3	2	6
Expertise	5	5	25
Impact	2	2	4
Project opportunity:			
Size	5	4	20
Complexity	5	5	25
Planning timescale	4	4	16
Quality of customer/supplier	1	2	2
External factors:			
Cultural fit	3	3	9
Quality of information	1	5	5
Demands of customer(s)	4	4	16
Environmental	3	3	9
Competitive position:			
Market strength	4	3	12
Proposed contract terms	4	4	16
	44	46	165
Total sum (wx)/sum (w)			3.59

In this case it is expertise and complexity, both at a maximum of 25, followed by size at 20, then planning timescale, demands of customers and proposed contract terms all at 16. Next in interpretation of the grid is the rationale behind the scoring for the highest risk factors. For this logistics project the high score for expertise was due to a lack of availability of skilled drivers in the area, and for complexity, the number of assumptions and pattern of drops. As the contract represented approximately 35 per cent of revenue for the relevant business unit, size was high risk due to the earnings at risk if the customer's demands were not met. These reasons were noted in a comments column on the spreadsheet to the right of the scores.

BDP RISK MAP

The glossary of terms used in Tables 3.1 and 3.2 is shown in full in the appendix to Chapter 3 and includes notes where there were obvious relationships between risks. This has been used to develop a risk map, shown in Figure 3.1, though the cognitive mapping method was not originally used in this example.

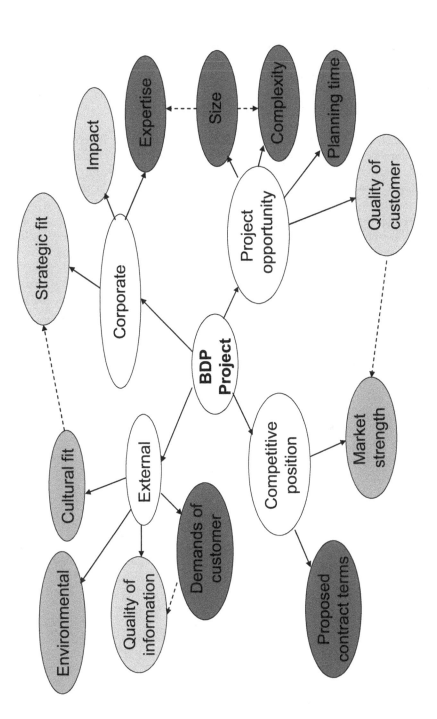

Figure 3.1　BDP risk map

This shows just some of the possible inter-relationships between risks represented by the dotted lines. Others are likely, but there is a limit as to how many can be shown without crossing the solid lines and making the map look too busy. The direction of the arrows does not necessarily imply cause leading to effect, but does indicate that a high risk in the first area may lead to or be linked in some way to the risk in the second area.

As the risk assessment in Table 3.2 shows the project was rated as above average risk (a score of 3.59 on a 5-point scale) it is not surprising to see almost half the ovals shaded in red (darkest shading) to highlight the priorities for action. According to the risk return matrix the company had in use at the time, the project return would need to be in excess of 18 per cent for this project to even be considered by the group board. With proposed contract terms being assessed as high risk, the opportunity to achieve a higher return through higher prices would be limited, making it unlikely that this project would be approved.

Even where the project does not gain approval, the time spent on risk assessment would not have been wasted. First, it may have saved the project going ahead with a poor chance of success, and second, it provided valuable learning for the business development team that could benefit future project appraisals.

APPENDIX TO CHAPTER 3 – GLOSSARY OF PROJECT RISK ATTRIBUTES

Strategic fit: the potential contribution to corporate goals as stated in the strategic plan (e.g. market segment penetration) of the project (1 = good fit, 5 = poor fit). See also cultural fit.

Expertise: the availability of knowledge and skills needed for the project to succeed, either existing or available to buy in (1 = relevant strength, 5 = relevant weakness). See also size and complexity.

Impact: the potential impact on the company's business, reputation or brand image which may derive from the project and related publicity, e.g. loss of business due to public sensitivity to product being carried or reputation of new customer (1 = positively enhancing, 3 = insensitive, 5 = sensitive and potentially damaging).

Size: the scale of the project relative to the existing business unit, indicated by capital expenditure, length of contract, human resources and annual revenue (1 = small, 5 = large).

Complexity: the number of variables or assumptions inherent in the project, which impacts on the company's ability to predict and manage the outcome, e.g. technical or process complexity (1 = simple, 5 = complex).

Planning timescale: the time available to research and develop a project proposal before a decision must be made (e.g. response to tender), and for the project to be implemented on time (1 = long, 5 = short).

Quality of customer: the profile of the prospective customer in terms of ownership, financial viability/stability, sustainability and commitment to existing market(s), e.g. credit rating (1 = good, 5 = poor). See also market strength.

Cultural fit: the potential match or mismatch in the values, beliefs and practices of the contracting parties in the project affecting customer relations (1 = good fit, 5 = poor fit).

Quality of information: the reliability, validity and sufficiency of base data and other relevant information available to form the basis for project assumptions and appraisal (1 = good, 5 = poor). See also demands of customer(s).

Demands of customer(s): the challenge posed by the customer's expectations, understanding, consistency and communication of their own service requirements, and the risk of the project not satisfying them (1 = barely demanding, 5 = highly demanding).

Environmental: the likely impact of political, legal, economic, social and technological factors on the project, e.g. asset obsolescence (1 = low, 5 = high).

Market strength: the position of the company relative to competitors, e.g. unique selling point for this project, or negotiating power with customer (1 = strong, 5 = weak).

Proposed contract terms: the evaluation of the likely contract terms, and potential to pass risk(s) to the customer(s) (1 = favourable, 5 = unfavourable).

Source: Adapted from Harris, 1999, p. 369–370

CHAPTER 4

SYSTEMS DEVELOPMENT PROJECTS

DEFINITION

Systems development projects, also known as infrastructure or IT projects, aim to improve or replace all or part of a business system. The system could be a business process control system or a financial/information/management system. The project might involve designing a new bespoke information system, or purchasing and implementing an off the shelf software solution. The new software might run on existing computers or networks or might require the purchase of new hardware, for example new servers and workstations.

CHARACTERISTICS

Systems development projects (SDP) were the most commonly experienced type of project in the cross-industry survey outlined in Chapter 1, with 70 per cent of responding managers having recent experience of this type of project. The system may be linked to production planning in a manufacturing environment, for example an enterprise resource planning (ERP) system, where compatibility with supplier and/or customer systems is important. It may be a financial information system where audit trail and verification are important. Users may be purely internal to the organization or the system could allow access by external parties, for example on on-line sales systems for customer order processing.

These projects are often characterized by the difficulty of communications needed between technology experts and non-technical users. Whilst an internal client or customer may be in the driving seat in terms of specifying the requirements, external parties may also need to use the system. The first problem that may arise is where the client does not fully understand the specification of solutions available, or their user needs. This can cause significant uncertainty at the outset, with project definition problems.

Prior to selection of a system provider and a signed contract, there may be a competitive tender process, or at the least a number of site visits and demonstrations. There could be an evaluation of options by prospective users, or some sort of trial before a decision is made. Once the new system is established, there may be extensive testing and training required before the system can actually operate 'live' and any existing system can be closed down.

Often the implementation stage where data from an existing system needs to be transferred to the new system without disruption to the service provision is the most difficult stage. Long gone are the days of extensive 'parallel' running in IT projects as this is rarely feasible with modern networked systems. Transition tends to be the most time critical stage of IT projects, and where much of the project risk crystallizes. Security of the system and disaster recovery is usually extremely important. Often some sort of support or maintenance contract is signed, whether or not the system is off the shelf or bespoke.

Whilst the first rule of project management is that every project is different, and with IT projects this is certainly evident, there is strong evidence of a high level of similarity in the reasons such projects fail. Indeed this is one of the most researched types of project in the project management literature, where reasons for project failure have been investigated.

SDP RISK ATTRIBUTES

Table 4.1 compares key project risk areas for IT projects from three recent studies, which are very similar even though the research context, country and methodologies differ.

In the first column, key risk attributes were drawn from a discussion that started with the participants' own risk factors identified for business development projects (BDP risks – see Chapter 3). The focus group discussions (facilitated by the researcher as part of a larger action research study) took place in the UK and Belgium and explored the similarities and differences between SDP and BDP projects. The results showed many similarities, but different priorities and details, reflected in the weightings used and rationales captured in risk assessment exercises. The six highest priority risk attributes for IT projects are shown above.

Baccarini, Salm and Love (2004) derived 27 IT project risk factors from prior research and conducted in-depth interviews with 18 IT professionals in Western Australia to obtain their views and ranking of the 27 risks. Column 2 shows the top six risks, not in priority order, but aligned to the risks identified by Harris (1999). They went on to identify risk treatment strategies for the top 10 risks, classified as risk reduction or transfer. These are synthesized, with data from other sources in Table 4.2.

Tesch, Kloppenborg and Frolick (2007) also began with a comparison of software project risks from prior literature to compile a list of 92 risk factors, grouped into nine risk categories. They conducted group discussions with 23 project management professionals attending a PMI event in the US, where participants ranked the 92 risks as of high, medium or low importance, thus reducing the detailed list to 70 factors. Then they asked groups to rank the detailed risk factors within each of the nine risk categories, to identify the key factors in each group, then to rank the categories. The top six risk categories are shown in column 3 above, with the top rated risk factors in brackets. The participants went on to identify avoidance and mitigation strategies, again synthesized into risk management strategies in Table 4.2.

Table 4.1   IT project risks

Harris	Baccarini, Salm and Love	Tesch, Kloppenborg and Frolick
Expertise (availability of requisite skills)	Personnel shortfalls (insufficient human resources)	Personnel and staffing (lack of staff with the right skills)
Planning timescale (insufficient time for project implementation)	Unreasonable project schedule and budget	Funding and scheduling (entire project must be budgeted at the outset)
Demands of customer (expectations, understanding, consistency and communication of own requirements)	Unrealistic expectations (salesperson oversold product) Continuous changes to requirements by client	Sponsorship/ ownership (inadequate top management commitment) Relationship management (fail to satisfy user expectations)
Quality of information (reliability, validity and sufficiency of base data) Complexity (number/ nature of project assumptions)	Incomplete requirements	Requirements (changes managed poorly) Scope (requirements ignored for sake of technology)
Quality of supplier (viability, reliability and sustainability)	Diminished window of opportunity due to late delivery of software	

SDP RISK MAP

Figure 4.1 shows a composite risk map, drawn from the risk attributes identified above. It shows all key risks, but not all inter-relationships between them as there are too many to consider in this simple diagram. There is value in such a simple

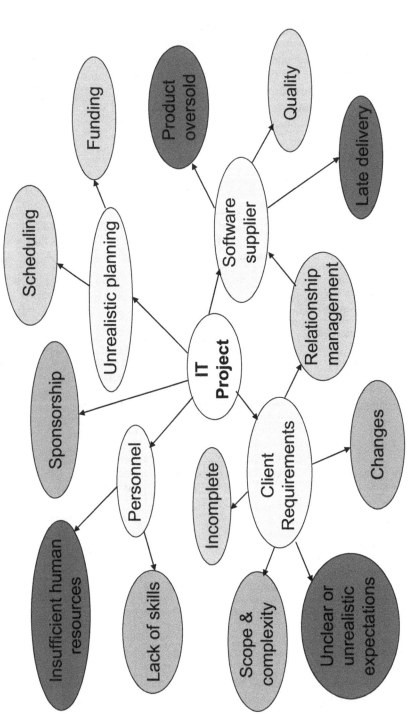

Figure 4.1   IT project risk map

representation for generic use for any IT project as a starting point for decision-makers and project teams to work from as a basis for discussion, assessment and for developing risk management strategies, prior to setting up a project risk register.

SDP RISK MANAGEMENT STRATEGIES

The project risks may be avoided, reduced or transferred to a third party by adopting a risk management strategy to address each key risk area. The suggestions summarized in Table 4.2 have been synthesized from those identified in the three research studies. Further explanation can be found in the published papers cited. In order to avoid any risks, the risk assessment and formulation of risk management strategies should take place as early as possible and before the organization has committed irrevocably to the project.

In many IT projects there may be multiple decision points such that stages can be managed and the project changed or aborted if risks appear too high, so as to outweigh the benefits of the project. Undertaking a feasibility study is an obvious example of a preliminary stage that may be carried out prior to deciding whether to go ahead and with which supplier or software product.

Sponsorship

It seems almost too obvious to state, but having a senior manager identified as the project sponsor who will champion the project and gain top management commitment to it can mean this risk is avoided, but does not always happen in IT projects. Perhaps it is due to the fact that IT projects occur in almost all organizations, including those where normal business is not project managed and therefore basic project management procedures are not followed.

Personnel and Staffing

The appointment or allocation of an experienced project manager to lead the project team is the first step, followed by a needs analysis for the skills required. If team members are to be selected on the basis of their skills and experience, they may then be found within the organization or may be trained in time to apply their new skills to the project. Otherwise new personnel might need to be recruited to fulfil project requirements. It may not be possible to foresee all competences required before the project is adequately defined and system and project team requirements are specified, so there are likely to be some ongoing training needs and some residual risk. Contingency plans might be needed to reduce the risk if key personnel become unavailable (e.g. through unexpected absence).

Client Requirements

In order to specify the project requirements, it is first necessary to identify what the system is expected to do and who will perceive whether objectives are met and whose needs are to be satisfied. So the first problem may be to identify the client(s) for an IT project. Is it the project sponsor, the internal system users or external system users? It may be obvious, such as in the on-line sales system example, where the firm's customers will use the system directly, but the system may need to be developed without actually referring to real customers at every step. It may be that the marketing department is the internal client in this example. In this case market research to increase awareness of customer needs is part of the risk management strategy.

Without knowing the capability of the software solutions available, it may be difficult to attain maximum clarity of client requirements at the outset, so a realistic time frame is needed to grow this task relevant knowledge. Where information is incomplete, strategies include a formal feasibility study, liaison with stakeholders, including potential suppliers, before an invitation to tender or shortlist is drawn up, thus gaining more information before a decision is made. Other strategies may be to ask stakeholders to prioritize desirable features and requirements and to manage expectations in terms of compromises that may be necessary to complete within time and budget.

Once requirements are reasonably specified, getting the client and sponsor to sign off the agreed requirements is essential in reducing the risk of costly changes. There should be clear consequences and deadlines for any changes identified later, and a formal change management process. This is perhaps more applicable to bespoke systems or packages that allow significant tailoring, but may not apply to all off the shelf solutions (where compromise is inherent in the product choice).

Ensuring good ongoing communications between the project team and the user(s) as well as with the supplier is one way to avoid or reduce the risk of user needs not being satisfied. Feedback on progress and test opportunities are obvious strategies, as is the plan to pilot test the new system in a small part of the organization before rolling out the solution to all ultimate users.

Software Supplier

The first strategy is to check out product claims by contacting the supplier's existing customers to get user feedback. Then check out the company's credentials, including a financial evaluation to reduce the risk of contracting with a supplier who is under-resourced. Demonstrations and testing of software solutions is normal practice before making payment commitments, and building in project review points (milestones) into the contract can mitigate supplier risk. Good communications can minimize the failure of the software to meet expectations, and progress reports can ensure that potential delays are flagged up early enough for action to be taken to keep the overall project on track.

Scheduling and Funding

At the outset of a project only rough estimates can be made of time and costs as the scope of the project and the system to be installed has not been fully specified. However, there may be useful guides, especially where other organizations have invested in similar systems, so trade press and associations may be useful sources of information. If the budget is imposed, then the functionality or optional features may have to be limited to stick to that budget. Trade-offs may need to be made between scope, time and cost to ensure that budgets can be met. Key skills in managing these risks are research, negotiation and monitoring.

This is not an exhaustive list of risk management strategies for IT projects, and many of them appear to be little more than sound business sense, but they are examples of best practice in project management, which many organizations still neglect in the everyday business practice. They are summarized in Table 4.2.

Table 4.2   IT project risk management strategies

Risk categories	Risk strategies
Sponsorship/ownership	Project sponsor to champion the project at top management level
Personnel and staffing	Appoint an experienced project manager Skills needs analysis Specific recruitment and selection Training and skills development Contingency planning for unexpected absence
Requirements	Stakeholder analysis Research and feasibility studies Prioritization of user needs Sign off of requirements by sponsor Agreed requirements change procedure Communications plan Pilot test phase
Software supplier	Customer feedback from existing users Credit reference (agency or own analysts) Demonstrations and testing Communications plan and milestones
Scheduling and funding	Clear requirements ascertainment Research and feasibility studies Trade-offs between scope, time and cost Negotiation and monitoring skills

CHAPTER 5

NEW SITE PROJECTS

DEFINITION

A new site is fairly self-explanatory, such projects may involve the choice of location, construction of a new building or refurbishment of an existing building. It may be a relocation project, where an existing building or site is to be vacated, or it could be an expansion project to accommodate new staff or new business. The new premises to be occupied might be purchased or leased. The scope of what is dealt with here does not include the construction itself, which would be undertaken by a property development company or building firm, but the acquisition of new business premises for any type of organization. If a construction company was building new premises for a client, then the project could be viewed as a new customer or business development project (BDP) from its perspective (see Chapter 3).

CHARACTERISTICS

The first characteristic is the selection of a suitable geographic location, then the choice of a specific site or premises. Considerations would therefore include the transport links, availability of nearby facilities for staff, for example nursery or crèche, shops, petrol stations, parking and the nature of the local environment (city, rural, residential or industrial). The project scope might include the acquisition of capital equipment for business operations and administrative purposes. Though investments in advanced manufacturing technology and major IT requirements are likely to be defined as separate or sub-projects.

The objectives of the move could be to gain more space, more flexibility, better quality, or lower rent or other relevant costs. It could be prompted by a business merger or acquisition (treated separately for risk assessment purposes) or a consolidation of operations. If it involves moving two streets away in the same town it will obviously be less complex than if the move is over a greater distance, especially cross-border into a country with a completely different language and culture. The organization may have a history of acquiring new sites on a regular basis, for example a supermarket or a hotel or restaurant chain, or it may be the only move it has or will experience.

The site could be an automated warehouse with minimal personnel involved, or it could be the nerve centre of a people oriented service organization or the company's administrative headquarters. The number and type of personnel involved is a key variable. If the relocation involves closing an old site some distance away from the new site, then extensive redundancy issues may pertain. The project may also be seen as part of a change management programme where staff morale may be affected by the choice and appearance of a new work environment.

Other complications might include a move to or from a heritage site, with the constraints of listed building regulations, for example the redevelopment of the British Museum site in Bloomsbury, London (Montague House dates back to 1676) following the relocation of the British Library in 1998 to a new purpose-built site in St Pancras. Moving or expanding operations on a green field or nearby a residential site might involve local protest and a lengthy public enquiry process, for example building a new terminal at London's Heathrow Airport (opened in 2008 after extensive delays).

Time pressures may impinge on the project, especially where the organization has already outgrown its present premises, or is under financial pressure to reduce premises costs. These project features will all have a bearing on the risks and management strategies needed for the project to succeed.

RELOCATION PROJECT RISK ATTRIBUTES

Since relocation is the most common and potentially complex of new site type projects, it is used for illustration purposes here. The example presented is the relocation from one part of the US to another, over 2,000 miles away, of an operational business unit of an engineering firm owned by a large multinational group with headquarters in the UK. The aim of the project was to consolidate manufacturing operations to improve efficiency and produce cost savings as part of a large-scale organizational restructuring. The two sites shortlisted were existing operational sites. The restructuring was managed by a relatively inexperienced change agent under considerable time pressure (just two months allowed for the move).

It is often helpful to conduct stakeholder analysis before considering the risks attached to any project, so this is shown in Figure 5.1. The analysis uses a power interest matrix (Mendelow, 1991 adapted by Johnson and Scholes, 1993, p. 177) to place stakeholder groups into four quadrants, which may then receive specified treatment. So, with the key groups, those with a high level of interest in the project and a high level of power in terms of their ability to impact on the outcome of the project, we have three groups of people who require close management by the project team. They are employees, managers and the HR department.

Stakeholder analysis

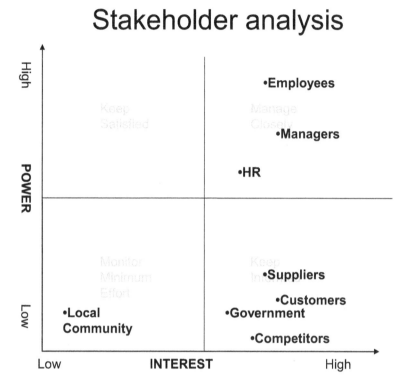

Figure 5.1   Relocation project stakeholders

Source: Adapted from unpublished MBA group coursework with permission

The risk attributes identified by organizational members for this project emphasize the role of the three key stakeholder groups.

Employees

Within this category there is a risk of losing employees through the move, with upside risk of them being poor performers and downside risk of them being valued and experienced high performers. There is then a risk of poor employee morale following the move, and a risk of the company not being able to fill vacancies due to a poor local labour market in one of the two shortlisted locations.

Management of Relocation

The absence of a dedicated and experienced project manager for the relocation exposed a leadership risk. This was closely linked to unrealistic scheduling, lack of understanding of implementation requirements and loss of confidence of personnel affected. It is not clear what role the HR department played in this project, but it may be assumed from the employee and management risks that the HR department missed an opportunity to mitigate those risks.

Continuity

The current installation projects underway could suffer from a lack of continuity of resources and management. Information transfer and changes to work practices could also threaten the success of operations before, during and after the move. Loss of project history, a knowledge management problem was also identified. Technology requirements in the new location and the physical transfer of equipment would delay completion (defined as the moment when the new site would be fully operational).

Organizational Impact

Integration of relocated with existing personnel, issues of organizational culture and weak business procedures were all expected to impact on the organization negatively, where if managed properly, they could have been enhanced (treated as upside risk).

Infrastructure Requirements

Unavailability of requisite office equipment meant that old equipment had to be transported long distance at high cost. Size of new building not properly scoped to ensure suitable for new hires, relocated and existing staff. The availability of suitable accommodation for relocated staff was limited by local housing market.

Costs – Budget Overspend

The risk areas for potential overspend were:

- capital costs – equipment, technology;
- removals – packing, transport and loss/damage to assets;
- legal and professional – lawyers, realty, consultancy, employment agency;
- human resources – temporary staff, recruitment and selection costs, training and incentive schemes;
- closure – redundancy, repairs and selling costs of old site/assets.

RELOCATION RISK MAP

The risk factors identified above are presented in Figure 5.2 in the form of a risk map, after the MBA group members involved in the live project undertook a class-

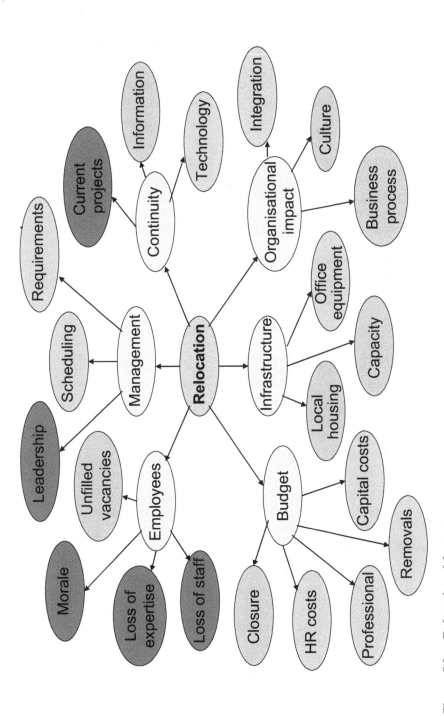

Figure 5.2   Relocation risk map

based exercise to map their risk constructs. It has been adapted to preserve their anonymity and that of the company.

The shading in the map reflects a risk assessment where the likelihood, impact and overall exposure to each risk were assessed on a high, medium, low basis. The map should be viewed as taking an employee perspective as it was drawn up by those directly affected by the project.

RELOCATION RISK MANAGEMENT STRATEGIES

Participants identified several mitigating actions in drawing up their first version of a project risk register, summarized for risks assessed as high and medium in Table 5.1 below.

Table 5.1   Mitigating actions

Source of risk	Mitigating actions
Employees Loss of staff	Offer positive and consistent benefits package
Loss of expertise	Negotiate key employees' benefits package to encourage move
Effect on morale	Good communications with staff and transparency of business case
Poor local labour market	Establish good market intelligence (before choice of location)
Management Leadership	Establish dedicated project management team with strong leader
Continuity Current projects	Maintain extra resources during move Flex project schedules for projects spanning relocation period
Organizational impact Culture	Use relocation as a catalyst for change, improve existing culture
Business procedures	Requires a development plan
Infrastructure Office equipment	Transport all office equipment from current site, reduce need for new
Capacity	Determine capacity required and ensure building completed in time

Source: Adapted from unpublished MBA group coursework with permission

CHAPTER 6

NEW PRODUCT DEVELOPMENT PROJECTS

DEFINITION

New product development (NPD), also known as innovation projects, start with an idea for a new product or service, which may come from a customer who perceives a need not currently served by the products available in the market, or from an established research and development (R&D) department. Indeed an NPD project can be seen as part of a programme of R&D, taking the idea and translating it into a marketable product. So when does a project stop being R&D and start becoming NPD? Well, there are many R&D projects that are really pure research, which may never materialize as new products, for example scientific projects in pharmaceuticals, perhaps due to lack of success in early trials (functionality) or lack of funding (if not seen as viable in terms of pricing and profit potential). NPD projects are closer to market than that, at what is referred to as the 'commercialization' stage, and must have a sound business case put forward to show viable sales and margins.

Innovation is defined as 'the use of new knowledge to offer a new product or service that customers want' (Afuah, 2003, p. 13). This implies that a certain amount of market research has already been conducted. Many companies have NPD projects without actually having a full scale R&D function, though some facility for product testing may be necessary to test out the prospect that customers do indeed want the new product in sufficient numbers and at a profitable price for the producer. NPD is well understood in manufacturing industries, such as food and consumer goods, but applies equally in a service context, for example new mortgage products in financial services.

CHARACTERISTICS

Many new products are not much more than old ones updated or enhanced in some way, though some involve completely new concepts. There is therefore variability in the level of novelty then that will impact on project risk. From a new recipe for supermarket brand chicken curry to a robotic vacuum cleaner, the key characteristic is that they must appeal to customers. The customers may be the general public for everyday consumables, or narrow market segments for specialized products, for example sports equipment, or sophisticated buyers in organizations that may wield considerable power in the marketplace. Knowing who your customers are and understanding what appeals to them is critical to the success of NPD projects.

Product development is by its nature very industry specific, so the nature of the product, delivery process and marketing will vary between industries. There may still be general issues or features of NPD that are widespread. The need for customer/consumer testing, for example, will apply equally to our chicken curry example (a panel of tasters) and our robotic vacuum cleaner (prototypes could be tested in the manufacturer's own offices), even to a new aircraft, which may be tested by pilots for their feedback as well as for functionality and safety.

The new product may work or produce the desired effects with a panel or small group, but the real challenge is often in estimation of volumes that might be demanded, prior to the product launch. Variation can be huge, between zero sales and an enthusiastic response where the new product flies off the shelves on the first day, for example a widely publicised new miracle face cream that knocks years off the wearer and despite a high price production cannot keep up.

NPD PROJECT CASES

For reasons of variation by industry, three quite different examples have been selected to illustrate the risks, before suggesting an approach to NPD project risk identification.

Food Processing

This prospective product applied a revolutionary process to an everyday raw vegetable, usually purchased all year round in a frozen state in the mass market, to enhance its freshness. Table 6.1 shows the perceived risks of commercialization and possible responses.

This particular product never reached the marketplace as legal issues proved insurmountable. However, the risk constructs may be sufficiently generic to re-use in other situations and match reasonably well with those found in other product development case studies (Harris and Woolley, 2009). The two cases reported by Harris and Woolley were named 'flavours' and 'carotene' and had similar project characteristics to the project evaluated in Table 6.1. 'Flavours' had five clusters of constructs labelled: business model; timing; market requirements; product viability; and technology. 'Carotene' had four clusters of constructs labelled: capacity; market response; scale up; and givens (product specification).

Table 6.1 Project risk attributes for NPD project

PROJECT RISK ATTRIBUTES	Responses to risk
CORPORATE FACTORS: 1 Strategic fit 2 Management capacity/availability 3 Expertise (technical/operations/selling) 4 Reputation	Share risk in joint venture Buy-in additional management Buy-in additional expertise
PROJECT: 5 Size (volume/throughput) 6 Cost structure/margins 7 Project timescale – product life cycle 8 Timing/readiness for launch 9 Technical complexity 10 Quality of information	Price at premium price (high margin) Improve quality of base case data
COMPETITIVE ADVANTAGE: 11 Protection of information 12 Competitors' response 13 Retailers' response 14 Attractiveness to bulk purchasers 15 Attractiveness to consumers	Patent (protection of process/know-how) } }Test market product }
OTHER/EXTERNAL: 16 Production site/location 17 Regulation (industrial/political)	Locate production outside UK

These fit well with corporate factors, especially constructs 2 and 3 (capacity and expertise), competitive advantage factors, especially 13 to 15 (attractiveness to market) and project factors, especially 5 (volume) and 10 (quality of information). The 'carotene' team identified consistency of product quality when entering the mass production process, which would also have been highly relevant in the case illustrated in Table 6.1.

Cosmetic Product

A new skin lightener product was developed in South Africa, where the project team worked with the researcher on mapping the risk and uncertainty. The result of the first mapping is shown in Figure 6.1

The original map was re-mapped over several iterations around the operating concepts. A later map is detailed in Figure 6.2. This map shows a greater number of risk attributes, but the clusters (users, market, manufacturing, supplier and resources) remain the same.

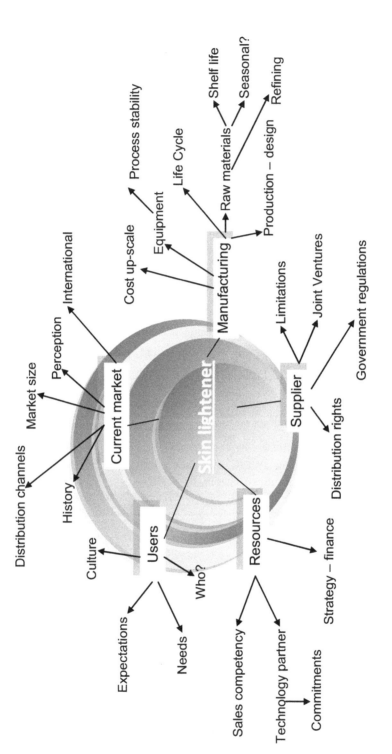

Figure 6.1   Early risk map – Skin lightener product
Source: Woolley (2004, p. 120)

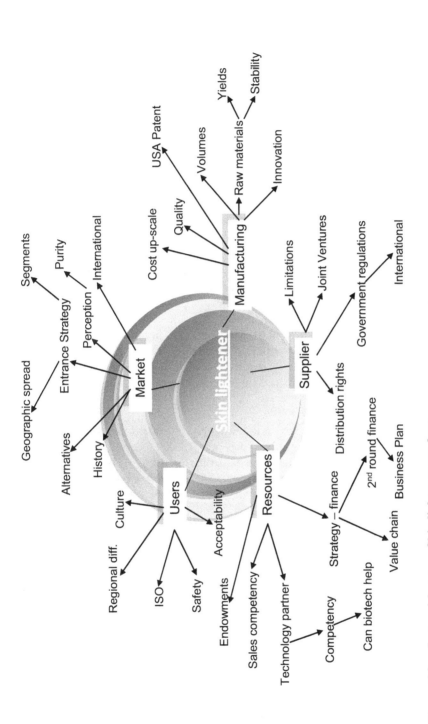

Figure 6.2   Later risk map – Skin lightener product

Source: Woolley (2004, p. 121)

All aspects of the value chain were discussed in the focus group and the task relevant knowledge developed significantly by knowledge sharing across the team. The new product development project progressed smoothly and was completed under time and under budget.

New Bachelor of Science (BSc) Degree

This curriculum development is an example of a NPD project in a UK university, where the peculiarities of the product or service is that it can only be sold once a year. This puts time pressure on the project to be completed on time to obtain a University Central Admissions System (UCAS) code in time for the new academic year. Whilst there is no national curriculum as such, the government's Quality Assurance Agency (QAA) produces subject benchmark statements in collaboration with subject associations (the academy).

For vocationally relevant degrees there is a need to determine employers' needs in terms of their expectations of what graduates should know and be able to do. There is also likely to be at least one relevant professional or statutory body that will regulate the learning outcomes for graduates who wish to become professionally qualified and work as practitioners. The number of stakeholder perspectives to consider in curriculum development leads to a risk that the new degree will not satisfy everyone's requirements and the new degree may not be validated in time or may not recruit target student numbers. Sources of risk are shown in Figure 6.3.

Whilst the risks in Figure 6.3 appear to be highly context specific, there is in fact a common structure to the clusters in that they are all stakeholders, indeed all directly involved in some way in the development of the product as parties in the value chain. The government might be seen as a customer from a funding perspective, the market may involve agents to recruit students. They are 'consumers' of the degree, with employers and the profession as end users.

NPD PROJECT RISK MANAGEMENT

From the cases illustrated it is suggested that value chain analysis may be the key to identifying sources of risk for NPD projects, at least at the strategic level, such that risk management strategies can be developed appropriately before the project is implemented. A summary of generic risk sources for NPD projects and risk management responses is shown in Table 6.2 (see page 62) using the value chain approach.

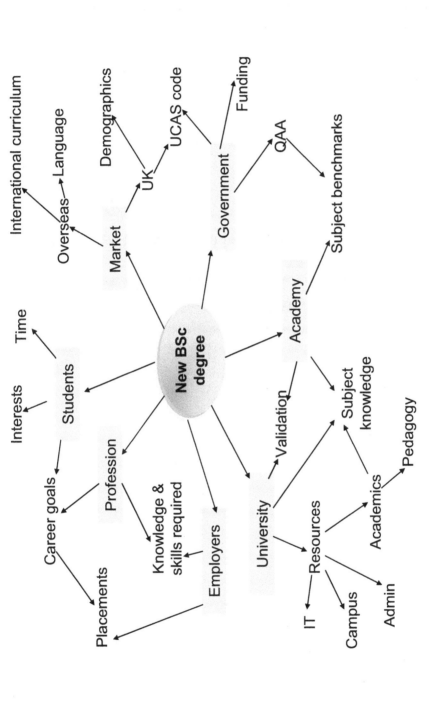

Figure 6.3 New BSc degree sources of risk

Table 6.2   Identifying and responding to NPD project risks

Sources of risk	Responses to risk
End users – expectations and aspirations	Establish preferences (market research) Product trials/testing
Customers – value proposition	Communications strategy
Market – distribution channels	Careful selection/briefing of agents Pricing strategy
Regulators – government, industry	Compliance monitoring/documentation
Manufacturers – delivery capability	Work planning/scheduling and monitoring
Suppliers – bought in goods and services	Clear requirements and selection/ negotiation
Designers – product specification	Feasibility study to test idea
Researchers – source of ideas, know-how	Protection by patents, copyrights, etc.

CHAPTER 7

BUSINESS ACQUISITIONS

DEFINITION

This type of project encompasses the purchase of all or part of an existing business undertaking, either by purchasing the operating assets or the shares. If it is a share purchase it could be 100 per cent to acquire a wholly-owned subsidiary, or a controlling interest (normally 50 per cent or more) in a company. They are also referred to as takeovers, where the acquiring organization is the bidder and the acquired business is referred to as the target. In the case of mergers, a more equal relationship is implied, where two or more parties agree to combine the business operations into a new structure.

CHARACTERISTICS

The factor that often determines the risk profile of the project is whether the acquisition or business combination is a 'friendly' agreement or not. If the owners of the target business put it up for sale, or otherwise cooperate effectively with the bidder's plan, they will normally supply more relevant information. If the takeover is 'hostile', where the board of the target company opposes the bid and recommends its shareholders to vote against it, the bidder will not have the same access to information. They will use publicly available information and market intelligence as the basis of formulating their bid. However, even in the case of a so-called 'friendly' sale, the board of the target company still has an obligation to its owners to negotiate the best price, so may provide and present information selectively to that aim. The quality of information in the hands of the bidder, therefore, has to be verified in some way.

Continuing with the 'friendly' scenario, the bidder would wish to establish whether and why the target business might be for sale. In the case of a small- or medium-sized enterprise it could be family owned by people who wish to retire or withdraw from business ownership. If it is part of a large group of companies it could be that it no longer fits with holding company strategy in terms of its business activities, or it could be sold to release funds for re-investment in another part of the group. It may be that the business for sale is unprofitable and would require a business recovery plan to turn it around. The rationale stated for the sale may be misleading or only part of the story. The caveat of 'Buyer Beware' is highly relevant even in an apparently friendly arrangement.

The motivation of the bidder may also vary, though often it is claimed to be for reasons of achieving economies of scale in the case of acquisitions within the same line of business. This benefit is rarely achieved post acquisition, especially in the short term. So why do so many such business acquisitions apparently fail to deliver? The underlying rationale might have been to acquire a competing business to eradicate the competition, or it might simply be 'empire building' on the part of the acquiring board or chief executive. The evidence from finance research suggests there are few cases where the bidder's initial profit forecasts are realized to the extent that bidder gains show up in the post-acquisition share price. This is often explained by the underestimation of change management costs to restructure business units and personnel and streamline operations. Productivity, especially in a service industry may be severely affected by lower staff morale and variation in working practices.

There are obvious areas of concern in terms of keeping existing customers satisfied and winning new business, especially where the business name and identity is changed. The costs of changing the business logos and marketing communications can be considerable, even where the name stays the same. Stakeholder communications is a key challenge for the acquiring project team. The impact of change is difficult to predict, especially where the general public is involved. Project managing a business acquisition is challenging for any team, but is one where specialist experience of successfully managing such projects before is a real and rare asset.

Measuring project success is difficult as actual business results can only be compared with estimates of what the outcomes would have been without the acquisition. Also, determining the end of the project can be problematic, in terms of drawing the line on post-acquisition implementation. The change management programme may be defined as a new project, so the focus here is on the pre-acquisition stage, taking the project from the idea through the decision to bid and at what price, the due diligence process, to the transfer of ownership.

PROJECT RISK ATTRIBUTES

Table 7.1 shows the risk attributes with brief definitions for business acquisitions in a large logistics company, based on the only four examples in the team's shared experience at the time. They were elicited using the repertory grid technique (Chapter 2) and group discussions and are detailed more fully in Harris (2007).

The full glossary of terms (Harris, 2007, p. 1065) included cross-references between constructs where participants found it difficult to have a conversation

Table 7.1   **Project risk attributes for business acquisitions**

Risk Attributes	Brief definition
1. Strategic location	Impact on logistics network coverage
2. Integration (with existing operations)	Potential benefit of merging operations
3. Familiarity with territory	Extent of own local knowledge
4. Size of target acquisition	Scale of acq. relative to existing operations
5. Timescale (to reap rewards)	Time to realize benefits of integration
6. Customer quality/continuity	Customer profile and market position of acq.
7. Environmental issues	Impact of acq. on PEST factors
8. Technology	State of IT systems in target company
9. Management ability (target business)	Knowledge, ability, motivation, continuity
10. Compatibility (of business culture)	Cultural fit of target company with own
11. Quality of information	Reliability, validity, sufficiency of base data
12. Acquisition type/terms	Share/asset valuations and likely bid price

Source: Adapted from Harris, 2007

about one risk factor without reference to another. The inter-relations are easier to present in the form of a cognitive map (shown below). Whilst the definitions of risk attributes 1, 2 and 8 relate specifically to the logistics industry, they could be redefined, and the other nine attributes could be applicable to other industries. The focus of the ninth attribute, management ability, was on the target company, but being new to managing business acquisitions, this was also a major risk for the bidding company. With the benefit of hindsight, the chief executive acknowledged this during a post project review meeting.

ACQUISITION RISK MAP

Figure 7.1 shows the risk attributes from Table 7.1 in visual form, after the team had reflected further on the risk assessment of the four acquisitions. Of the four cases, one was assets only and three by shares, of which two had been cross-border acquisitions of companies located in mainland Europe in new territory for the UK-owned group. The map was produced as an aide-memoire to guide any further acquisitions, though no more such projects took place during the period of the research.

The map does not strictly follow the oval mapping technique as described in Chapter 2 as it does not place the name of the project in the centre of the page. It starts with the first and most important risk attribute in the logistics business, that of the strategic

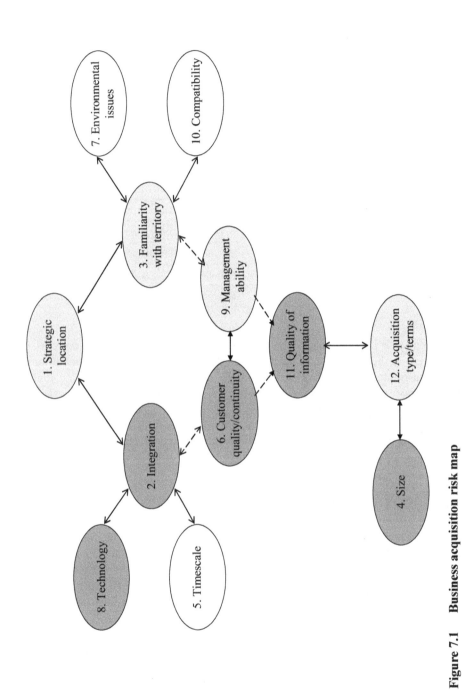

Figure 7.1 Business acquisition risk map
Source: Harris (2007, p. 1069)

location of the target business, and maps other attributes from there. The reason the map is drawn this way is that it was not used to derive the risk attributes (they were found by using the repertory grid technique), but it was drawn up later as a visual representation of risks previously identified, highlighting their interconnectedness. The use of two-way arrows for most of the links indicates that the risk in one area can impact on the other and vice versa. The dotted lines indicate that the relationship between risk areas is less strong than those joined by solid lines.

RISK MANAGEMENT STRATEGIES

Taking the same 12 risk attributes, with a more generic definition of strategic location, applicable to any business, strategies for reducing the downside risk and/ or exploiting the upside risk are suggested in Table 7.2.

Table 7.2   Project risk management strategies for business acquisitions

Risk Attributes	Risk Management Strategies
1. Strategic location (in relation to customers, supplies/resources, local labour market, corporate headquarters and existing operations)	+ Expand customer base in new area or reduce operating costs by using cheaper resources - Dispose of distant sites and focus on near sites monitor extra travel costs post-acquisition
2. Integration (with existing operations)	+ Exploit opportunities to consolidate Review and update work practices
3. Familiarity with territory	Appoint an agent/adviser with local knowledge Recruit competent local managers
4. Size of target acquisition	Sell off non-essential parts of business to reduce potential borrowing and cost of servicing debt
5. Timescale (to reap rewards)	Specify implementation plan early
6. Customer quality/continuity	Marketing communications and incentives plan
7. Environmental issues	PEST and stakeholder analysis
8. Technology	Define systems requirements and IT projects
9. Management ability (target business)	Contracts with incentives for best managers Second temporary management from HQ
10. Compatibility (of business culture)	Appoint change management agent and consult
11. Quality of information	Due diligence process to verify information
12. Acquisition type/terms	Audit valuations and assess financial risks

CHAPTER 8

COMPLIANCE PROJECTS

DEFINITION

This type of project differs from those discussed so far as it arises from a requirement to do something, imposed by government or an external regulatory body, not as a matter of choice for the organization. Obvious examples are new legislation affecting all organizations in a certain jurisdiction, like employment laws, and organizations in a certain industry, like food labelling laws applicable to retailers. Compliance is not always seen as a project in this situation, but if the change is fundamental such that work practices have to change in order to comply, then increasingly organizations are defining such changes as projects and managing the change through project management.

Other statutory, professional or regulatory bodies may impose mandatory or advisory changes that some organizations have to have, for example medical profession, audit and financial services, or have chosen to have, for example ISO certification, accreditation or quality Kitemarks. This kind of scenario may only result in the definition of a project if it gives rise to a strategic or fundamental change. Whilst on occasions there is no choice about whether to comply, there are often choices to be made in terms of how to comply. Therefore options may still be formulated and evaluated before the decision is made that will lead to specification of the project requirements.

CHARACTERISTICS

Due to the imposed nature of this type of project, the first challenge is to identify the need and understand the requirements being introduced. In the case of commercial legislation this may be the responsibility of a legal department, but since such teams are often based at organizational headquarters, it may also be the responsibility of regional boards or management teams to identify local requirements, especially in multinational corporations. Companies of any size may employ specialist advisers to alert management to prospective changes, or to advise on best practice responses to new legislation, for example specialists on patents, employment, property, taxation, etc. The contracting out to professional consultants to manage the compliance may transfer all or part of the risk, but may not avoid all of the risk.

If the change is made by government, there is often extensive news coverage and publicity to alert the general public as well as business owners, so it is possible for some stakeholder groups to have earlier, better or distorted information before the organization has fully assessed the implications. This raises communications issues and matters of governance, in terms of how widely the organization needs to raise awareness of the changes and consult on implementation. Usually it is obvious which stakeholder group(s) will be most affected, for example employees in the case of new employment law, and consumers in the case of new food purity regulations. The aim of such legislation is protection of a sector of society, or the wider environment. In the current climate, there is an increasing amount of such legislation in the developed world, which some organizations are turning to their advantage by claiming to go beyond the legal requirements in their governance and corporate social responsibility.

Another feature that differentiates compliance projects is the severity of the consequences of not delivering the project on time. Whereas delay in most projects covered earlier might result in loss of business or financial penalties, delay in compliance, effectively non-compliance, could have disastrous consequences. For example non-compliance with standards might result in partners being struck off and denied a future professional career. Non-compliance with health and safety legislation could lead to officers or employees of the organization being held personally liable and even imprisoned, especially where members of the public suffer death or injury as a result. This could be the ultimate impact of not managing the downside risk. Most managers would agree that in a risk assessment this sort of impact would go off the scale! In cases where consequences of non-compliance are potentially extreme, there is usually a good deal of time and guidance available prior to the regulation taking effect for organizations to prepare themselves.

PROJECT RISK ATTRIBUTES

Table 8.1 shows the main risk areas identified for a compliance project to adopt new professional standards. The example is drawn from the accountancy profession, but would be applicable across a range of contexts.

These risk attributes can be clustered into broad areas of knowledge, resources and quality, which might typify the compliance risk areas in any professional services organization. Most of the project risk attributes would also apply to other compliance projects, such as health and safety legislation, though some definitions might vary.

Table 8.1   Compliance project risks

Project risk attribute	Definition
1. Identification	Alertness to professional development of new standards
2. Understanding	Understanding the impact of new standards
3. Expertise	Specialist knowledge required
4. Awareness	People across the organization who need to know
5. Competence	Skills needed to manage the change
6. Capacity	Human resources available to manage the change
7. Costs	Availability of funding required
8. Systems	Need for new/updated systems to cope with change
9. Suppliers	Need for new materials or other input from suppliers
10. Time	Ability to meet deadline for compliance
11. Certification	Will changes satisfy regulatory body?
12. Quality	Will changes satisfy other stakeholders, e.g. clients?

RISK MAP

The above example is presented visually in Figure 8.1, with the project risk attributes clustered into three main areas. Where professional and statutory bodies (PSBs) have an advisory role as well as a regulatory one, they might produce this sort of analysis in the form of guidance documents available to their licensed practitioner members through member services. PSBs might also provide or recommend relevant continuing professional development (CPD) events, to develop both technical expertise and managerial competence.

The dotted lines show where one risk attribute might impact on another. For example if a firm is slow in identifying professional developments likely to bring about new or revised standards or procedures, then there will be less time available for the firm to prepare. Also, personnel responsible for identification of new regulations may have the research skills required but not the capacity in terms of the time needed to perform this role.

RISK MANAGEMENT STRATEGIES

The example in Table 8.2 is drawn from professional services experience, where the tendency may be to view regulation and compliance as something of a nuisance is

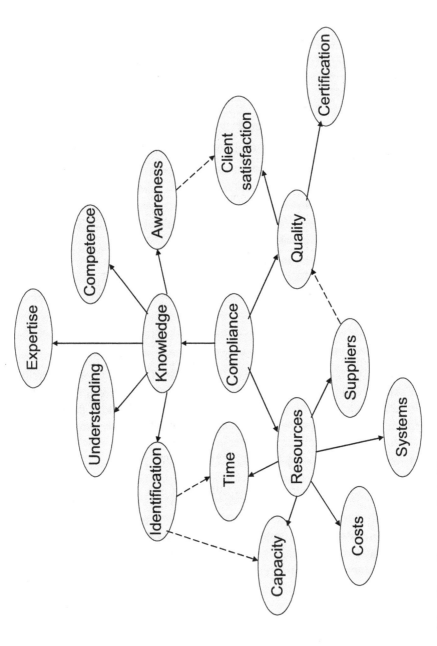

Figure 8.1   Compliance project risk map

Table 8.2   Compliance project risk management strategies

Project risk attribute	Risk management strategies
1. Identification (of need to change)	Identify personnel responsible for spotting changes in legal/professional rules, and scanning newspapers, trade journals, economic and political digests
2. Understanding (requirements)	Relevant CPD (technical) and professional guides
3. Expertise (to address needs)	Consult specialist advisers, professional bodies, etc.
4. Awareness (across organization)	Communications strategy
5. Competence (to manage change)	Managerial CPD
6. Capacity	Temporary staff or secondments
7. Costs	Save costs elsewhere in budget, borrow or increase professional fees (pass extra costs on)
8. Systems	IT project to upgrade systems
9. Suppliers	Inform suppliers and source alternatives
10. Time	Project scheduling and critical path analysis
11. Certification	Compliance verification prior to deadline
12. Quality	Client communications and feedback analysis

certainly treated as a negative kind of risk in terms of risk management. However, other examples may be viewed far more positively as an opportunity, especially by the market leader in the industry. The example in Figure 8.1 of food labelling regulation has been viewed as an opportunity by J Sainsbury plc, claiming it is not just compliant but actually influenced the new regulation by leading in this area of food packaging and consumer information in its supermarket business. Managing risk as opportunity in this way means that publicity is vital to increase sales sufficiently to cover any costs of compliance and increase profits.

The risk (opportunity) management strategy in this case involved extensive merchandising and advertising, which costs money but can have enormous benefits. The use of celebrity chef Jamie Oliver in its advertising campaign to promote J Sainsbury plc as the best choice of supermarket for those interested in healthy eating is a compelling example, piggybacking on his well publicised 'Ministry of Food' campaign.

In this case the fourth risk management strategy in Table 8.2 would not just be an internal communications strategy, but a marketing communications strategy to cash in on this positively framed risk. This example might give managers in other industries some food for thought on turning project risks into business opportunities.

CHAPTER 9

EVENT MANAGEMENT

DEFINITION

The definition of an event-type project is the staging of something important that will happen at a fixed time in future and attract people to attend as participants and/or spectators. The term 'event' is used specifically in sport, for example in the programme for athletics. Other type of events like an art exhibition or a music festival might be part of a tour or seasonal programme. Theatre productions, opera or ballet performances may be defined as events or may be normal business operations for a specialist entertainment company. For performances to be defined as events they would be expected to be more unique in some way. Fundraising or charity events can be defined as one-off events for project management purposes, even if they are repeated as annual events. The participants, performers, hosts, venue could all be different, so making each event unique in some way. Many events-type projects are found in the public sector or not-for-profit sector, but all organizations might have events to manage, such as product launches, hospitality or corporate conferences and workshops.

CHARACTERISTICS

The main characteristic is that of a fixed time being set to stage an event well ahead of time, where delays in project delivery just cannot happen. The time constraint for preparing for the event is critical, so realistic work scheduling and time management are crucial. The most complex of events such as staging the Olympics, involving the construction of a whole village, new sports facilities, transport infrastructure, coordination of more contracts than most companies manage in a lifetime, requires an incredible lead time of more than five years. Still, most cities that host the Olympics experience such time delays on elements of the project that threaten the preparations being ready on time and cause huge budget overspends to fix.

The number and diversity of stakeholders for most major sports events will pose significant risks. When added to that, the success or failure will be shown up internationally by the world's media, it may bring into question whether it is too big a challenge for the tools of project management. The risks involved can be so great that it raises the question as to why so many cities (most with limited relevant experience) want to bid to host the event and whether their decision-making is rational (Emery, 2002). The main reason stated by bidders is that staging the event can bring with it huge investment which will bring economic benefits to the region. However, it is suspected that the attraction of publicity and media attention is the main reason bidders want to host the games, to raise the profile of their city.

Other less high profile events such as organizing an international conference may seem less complex due to the much smaller scale of the event, but the elements of complexity (organizational, technical, human behavioural and financial) still provide a range of risk areas to be managed. With most event-type projects the first question to address is why are we doing this? Is the main aim to raise funds, profile, to share knowledge, provide networking opportunities? The next question is the target number and location of attendees (which is likely to determine venue options) and what will attract them to attend. In the case of an internal management conference attendees may not have a choice, it may be an expectation.

PROJECT RISK ATTRIBUTES

Risk attributes are likely to be quite context-specific for events compared to other project types, so there will be significant variation at the detailed level. The analysis in Table 9.1 is therefore restricted to the top (strategic) level initially, which is then developed further for two examples, a major sports event and an academic conference in Table 9.2.

Each source of risk may be broken down into more detailed risk attributes. Table 9.2 shows more detail for a major sports event and for an academic conference. The sources of risk are very similar for the two different examples, it is the level of risk that differs considerably, mainly due to the scale of the project, and therefore the extent of risk management required.

RISK MAP

Figure 9.1 shows a cognitive map drawn up by the secretary of a subject association, acting in the role of project manager for an international conference (held every three years) with three professional body sponsors, two university partners/venues, a doctoral student colloquium and a social programme, for just over 100 delegates. It was held in Paris, managed from the UK with support from the host institutions and a small scientific committee. Participants came from more than 10 countries, mostly European, but all documents and presentations were in English.

Delegates were given accommodation information and asked to make their own bookings. A conference fee was payable (in euros or sterling, so there was some

Table 9.1   Project risk attributes – strategic level

Sources of risk	Definition (generic)
Size	Scope, number of contracting parties, number of attendees, number of countries involved, number of venues, duration of event
Host organization	Core business and competencies, corporate culture, politics, experience of similar events
Human resources	Availability and expertise of personnel, training needs and use of volunteer (untrained, low paid) labour
Funding	Self-funding expectation or external funding required, commercial or professional sponsorship
Complexity	Demands of technical requirements and coordination of multiple parties
Diversity	Propensity for conflict between stakeholder interests
Venue(s)	Security, capacity, accident and emergency facilities, disaster recovery
Timescale	Realism in planning time and project pressure points
Publicity	Amount and nature of media attention. Impact on image

Table 9.2   Project risk attributes – major sports event and academic conference examples

Sources of risk	Major sports event	Academic conference
Size/scope	No. of athletes, spectators, contracts, countries, sports governing bodies, duration (weeks)	No. of papers, tracks, presenters, participants, exhibitors, duration (days)
Organization	Local government-type organization, politics, limited knowledge and experience	Voluntary-type organisation (no professional/admin staff), but with some relevant experience
Human resources	Relevant professional credibility, team experience, volunteers	All part-time volunteers (mostly unpaid)
Funding	Government/commercial/ temporary	Self-funding/professional bodies
Complexity	Multiple parties/languages/venues	All English speaking
Diversity	Multiple stakeholder perspectives, including local community	Mostly controllable by scientific committee
Venue(s)	Indoor/outdoor venues spread around	Hotel/conference/social venue(s)
Timescale	Long range planning cycle	Annual planning cycle
Publicity	Full range of media, high publicity	Purely web-based, little outside interest

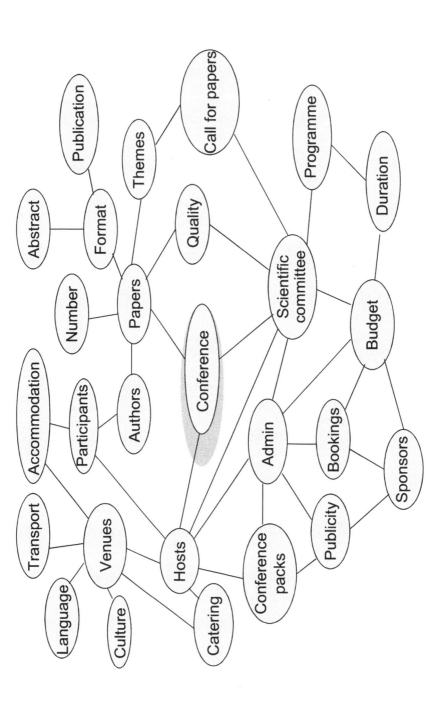

Figure 9.1 Risk map for international conference

exchange risk). The project was ready on time (in terms of conference packs, venue and programme preparation), it made a small surplus (against a break-even target) and was successful in terms of both attendance and feedback. This was achieved in the month of September, despite it being holiday time in the two months leading up to the event date (French national holiday time is August and academics take leave during July as well). The risks were mainly controllable, and the only formal risk discussed by the board was to ensure that the risk posed by holding the conference dinner on a river boat (in the event of an accident) belonged to the boat operator (who was assured to be appropriately insured for public liability).

RISK MANAGEMENT STRATEGIES

Returning to the generic project risks, risk management strategies are suggested in Table 9.3.

Table 9.3   Events management risk strategies

Sources of risk	Risk management strategies
Size	Limit scope by minimizing the number of parties and contracts Ensure capacity is available to accommodate numbers and manage process Divide main project into smaller projects or work packages to manage
Organization	Knowledge management, draw on experience/expertise
Human resources	Recruitment of suitable temporary personnel earlier than required Ensure training needs are met for permanent, temporary and volunteer staff Appoint leader and team members to project manage event
Funding	Bid for maximum government, commercial and sponsorship funding Scenario analysis and budget for contingency plans
Complexity	Consult experts to prepare technical specifications Research participant requirements Define specialist projects or work packages to manage Build a model to simulate complex processes and test sensitivity
Diversity	Analyze stakeholder interests and formulate management strategies Ensure project team leader is capable of conflict resolution
Venue(s)	Test security, accident and emergency, disaster recovery arrangements Contract out accommodation bookings and vet all subcontractors Public liability insurance
Timescale	If unrealistic timescale at start, consider withdrawal or alter event date Scheduling and critical path analysis. Time management skills
Publicity	Pass risk to specialist agency to manage opportunities and risks

PART 3
PROJECT RISK MANAGEMENT POST-DECISION

CHAPTER 10

PROJECT RISK MANAGEMENT

In Part 2 case illustrations and examples were used to identify project risks and to suggest risk management strategies for seven different types of project. This chapter draws together the common themes for identifying risks and formulating strategies in each type of project. This chapter starts by reviewing the framework for project risk management contained in the PMBOK® (PMI, 2008, p. 274) and suggesting a checklist of inputs to project risk identification. The timing of risk management is then considered, followed by the tracking of results through the use of risk registers (risk monitoring and control). Finally, a framework derived from case research to integrate risk management and project management with other strategic management functions is presented and discussed.

FRAMEWORK FOR IDENTIFYING SOURCES OF PROJECT RISK

The process set out in the PMBOK® follows six steps for project risk management:

1. risk management planning;
2. risk identification;
3. qualitative risk analysis;
4. quantitative risk analysis;
5. risk response planning;
6. risk monitoring and control.

The first two steps are about understanding the scope of the project and the likely sources of risk, which start out as uncertainties at the pre-decision stage. The following analysis can help to suggest tools to stimulate discussion about the possible sources of risk, preferably with one or all of the methods suggested in Chapter 2, though this is not essential.

Business Development Projects

The strategic analysis of the organizational and environmental context for the project can help to generate several possible risks. First, the analysis of strengths, weaknesses, opportunities and threats (SWOT) can identify risk areas for the organization from internal and external perspectives, and help to analyze the strategic fit of the project. Then a more detailed analysis of the external factors, political, economic, social, technical, legal and environmental (PESTLE) can identify further risk areas which may impact on the project.

If we consider the BDP risk attributes drawn from the case example in Chapter 3, using the repertory grid technique, SWOT and PESTLE analysis could well have revealed the first three (corporate) and last three (external and competitive) factors, half of the set of 12. Others were more about the project opportunity itself and parties to it. The invitation to tender might lead to identifying those in a BDP project.

Systems Development Projects

For an IT project, which is essentially a supply problem, the chain from software supplier to client (users) via sponsor (owner) can reveal half of the sources of risk found in Chapter 4 (page 42). The functional requirements of the system are defined by the client, and the risks here may determine whether the client is satisfied that the system does what it is supposed to do.

The focus here is on the quality dimensions (client and user satisfaction, functionality, benefits, etc.) of the success factors of project management. Time and cost dimensions are also relevant in this type of project in terms of scheduling (time) and funding (budget).

New Site Projects

In the relocation example, stakeholder analysis revealed key groups of people who need managing closely in a new site project. The employees are the principal group, followed by management and customers (continuity). These account for half of the risks found in Chapter 5 (page 54), with budget and scheduling and organizational factors accounting for most of the others, except infrastructure (geographic factors revealed by the PESTLE).

New Product Development (NPD) Projects

In contrast to the supply chain analysis used in IT projects, which focuses on the supply side (as the customer is assumed to be internal), analysis of the full value chain is appropriate in the NPD examples analyzed in Chapter 6 (page 57). Eight parties were identified in the value chain for NPD projects, though two of the three examples were involved in manufacturing products, so there could be fewer for service contexts.

Business Acquisition Projects

The project risks in acquisitions found in Chapter 7 (page 65) are similar to those from combining a BDP with a new site, so could largely be revealed from SWOT, PESTLE and stakeholder analysis, again adding to the constraints of time (attribute 5 timescale), budget (attribute 12 valuation) and quality (attribute 2 integration). Compatibility (attribute 10) is specific to business combinations, but could also apply to internal restructuring (relocation example).

Compliance Projects

The need for a compliance project could be identified through an organizational SWOT and PESTLE analysis, as new legislation or regulation should be identified as an opportunity or threat, but when we examine the nature of the risks for this project type (Chapter 8, page 71) it is mostly about managerial and professional competence and the knowledge management capability of the organization.

Event Management Projects

The nature of events varies widely, but the generic project risks identified in Chapter 9 (page 77) can largely be revealed by stakeholder analysis, with the key groups being the participants (competitors, spectators, performers or presenters) and personnel, venue issues, and again the traditional project constraints (time, budget and quality).

Checklist of Inputs for Project Risk Identification

From the above, it can be seen that a combination of business analysis tools can provide a useful start point for the identification of project risks:

- SWOT and PESTLE analysis;
- supply chain analysis;
- stakeholder analysis;
- value chain analysis;
- constraint analysis (time, budget, quality);
- ITT or project scope/requirements document analysis;
- competence or capability analysis (if not covered by SWOT).

TIMING OF RISK MANAGEMENT STEPS

It is likely that the opportunity to actively manage risks is greatest at the start of a project, often before any firm commitment is made to proceed with the project. This is why Chapter 2 advocates starting risk management early by identifying, assessing and formulating responses to key project risk attributes (steps 1 to 5 in the PMI structure set out in Chapter 10) prior to the decision to undertake the project, as part of the business case or project proposal. Assessment of strategic level risks at the pre-decision stage should inform both the project appraisal for the investment decision and the post-decision project management.

In the life cycle of a project in project management literature, the assumption is often made that the project already has the green light from the corporate board. In practice the project may well start with a feasibility study or other pre-implementation stage, such that the project may be aborted or redefined before the commitment is made to progress to implementation. In very large projects there may be multiple decision points or stage-gates when the project could be aborted or redefined.

The further the project progresses the less opportunity there will be to abort or redefine, or to implement some risk management strategies. For example the appointment of an experienced project leader (seen as a risk management strategy for IT projects in Chapter 4) needs to be done at the start, though if the leader leaves the organization or a more suitable candidate becomes available the leadership might change mid-project. Most risk management strategies, such as relevant training and development are best started early, and the benefits derived from such strategies if undertaken later diminish with time.

Chapter 1 set out a process model of strategic investment appraisal for business development projects (Figure 1.1, page 10). This depicts a bottom-up process of identifying project opportunities, in a divisionalized organization, where the ideas are generated and defined at business unit level. With invitations to tender (ITTs) for most logistics business this was invariably the case. The diagram implies that the group board's first knowledge of the opportunity was after a full business case had been worked up and agreed at divisional level (stages 2 to 5), immediately prior to the decision to fund the project or not (stage 6).

In fact, divisional managers were required to alert the board to significant projects at the early screening stage (stage 3), where the score for size in the early risk assessment could trigger such reporting. Whilst training and development exercises in the case organization often assessed projects at a later stage (to ensure adequate knowledge of the risks), the user guide advocated its use at stage 3 to achieve the most benefits (reflected in the feedback). Teams were then encouraged to update the grid (both scores and narratives) before submitting the case to the board at stage 6, and to review it at stage 7 as part of the post-audit process. Where used at least three times in the project's development, early screening, board decision and post-audit review, the benefits of project risk assessment as a dynamic tool could be fully realized.

In later use of the project risk assessment grid in this case organization, the project risk attributes were reviewed and changes made to identify a smaller number of risk attributes of importance post-decision, where there would be the most scope for risk management strategies. These ongoing project risk factors were also identified in order to build a more formal link with key performance indicators (KPIs) for monitoring and control during implementation and to inform the project review process. Five such factors were identified as:

1. expertise (action taken to identify and remedy shortages);
2. customer relations (managing the demands of the customer);
3. environmental factors (seen as more of an amalgamation of possible operational risks that might require mitigating action to minimize the effect, even where the risk was seen as low overall);
4. quality of information (where this can be weak prior to the decision point, it may include assumptions that need revisiting in order to manage the project within budget);
5. complexity (mostly technical challenges).

Other changes to the original set of attributes identified in the logistics case were:

• To delete the first attribute 'strategic fit' as it caused a lot of debate for very little value, since all projects being assessed were being given low scores as they were all considered to be a good fit with the strategy (or they would not be considered). It was not an operational construct, but a corporate construct which had served its purpose as a group discussion prompt back in the days when the strategy was less clear. It was difficult to verify its inclusion based on current risk literature.
• To focus more attention on the key operational risk areas by changing the order and clustering of the remaining risk attributes.

This resulted in the 10 risk attributes grouped into five pre-decision and five post-decision shown in Table 10.1 (page 88). The other 'casualties' in addition to strategic fit were impact (image/reputation) and cultural fit. These were rarely assessed as high risk, had medium/low weightings, and were seen as either unimportant or even diluting the overall risk score.

This reflected the outcome of group discussions facilitated by the researcher around the concept of controllability. The five risk attributes in the top section labelled pre-decision factors were agreed as factors that could not easily change once the project was approved and contracts signed, or (in the case of project scheduling) that most of the control was at the project planning stage. The size and scope of the business, terms and conditions and the deadline for delivery crystallized at that point. It was agreed for BDP projects that these factors need not be re-assessed in

Table 10.1   BDP controllability and timing of risk management responses

RISK ATTRIBUTES	RISK MANAGEMENT RESPONSES
Pre-decision factors:	
Size Planning timescale Quality of customer Market strength Proposed contract terms	Understanding capability, knowing limits/feasibility Scheduling and project planning Credit checking, evaluating financial statements Competitor analysis and negotiation Pricing and risk sharing
Key ongoing factors:	
Complexity Expertise Quality of information Demands of customer(s) Environmental impact	Modelling/testing the business process (advanced IT) Buy in or training and development Research and information sharing Customer relationship management Research and awareness

all project reviews, though some re-assessment might continue in training exercises in order to learn more generally about risk assessment.

The detailed risks in the other two areas, market strength and quality of customer could arguably change post-decision, but it would be too late to change contract terms until the period of the contract expired and contract renewal was considered (as a new project proposal). Only the key ongoing factors would therefore be re-assessed as the project progressed. It is suggested that these should be expanded and developed by the project team into detailed aspects, especially complexity, information quality and demands of customer(s) where the risks were higher, for monitoring through a risk register. For other types of project there could be more opportunity to continue taking action to manage all of the project risks.

RISK MANAGEMENT STRATEGIES

For each type of project considered in Part 2, between 10 and 20 risk management strategies have been identified, totalling 100. These have been analyzed and the following six categories emerge, in the order of frequency of observation:

1. project management (PM) 23 per cent;
2. human resource management (HR) 21 per cent;
3. stakeholder management (SM) 19 per cent;
4. knowledge management (KM) 18 per cent;
5. financial management (FM) 10 per cent;
6. trials or pilot testing (TT) 9 per cent.

Project Management

This category includes the deployment of project management methodologies and techniques such as work breakdown structure, scheduling, critical path analysis, etc. and the establishment of a project leader and project team. The most observations for this type of risk management strategy were in IT projects, relocation and events management, where timing is critical. The lower frequency for business and product development may also reflect the fact that they are considered as everyday projects where business processes and project management are well-developed and therefore not rated as high risk (perhaps project management is a given or a strength). It was certainly noted that many IT projects fail due to inadequate project management, and that events are not always managed by competent project managers.

Human Resource Management

This category includes recruitment, training and development of personnel, including managers and the management of change in work practices. This type of strategy featured most strongly in acquisitions, IT projects and relocation. Again it did not feature much or at all in business and new product development projects.

Stakeholder Management

This category includes stakeholder analysis and management through consultation, relationship management and communications. It featured most strongly in software development projects, NPD projects and events management, all of which must be very customer-focused. However, business development projects are almost completely customer-focused, but only featured twice in a set of 10 risk strategies. It may be that the focus is only on customers and few other stakeholder groups present high risks. In IT projects and events management there are many more stakeholder groups with diverse interests to manage.

Knowledge Management

This category includes searching for information, recording, analyzing, sharing and documenting information, for example in market research and feasibility studies. It features most strongly in BDP and NPD projects and in acquisitions. It is closely related to training and development, so overlaps with that aspect of HR management. When combined these two strategies feature strongly in compliance projects.

Financial Management

This category includes credit checking of suppliers and customers, financial modelling and budget management as well as business valuation, pricing strategies and contract terms. It is no surprise that it features most in business acquisitions, where a high level of financial expertise is required, and next in BDPs where terms are agreed and new customers vetted.

Trials and Pilot Testing

This category includes testing ideas at the feasibility study stage, testing possible solutions and new products. This could be clinical trials in pharmaceuticals, tasting panels with new food products or system testing in IT products, so features most strongly in IT and NPD projects.

PROJECT RISK MONITORING AND CONTROL

Risk registers are now in common use for recording and tracking risk assessment and risk management strategies and actions. Typically they are set out in tabular form in a spreadsheet with headings for:

- reference number;
- description of risk (following breakdown of each risk area from strategic to operational level risks, sometimes described as risk events);
- risk assessment – probability or likelihood (chance of this event impacting on the project);
- risk assessment – potential outcome or impact (severity of impact on the project);
- overall assessment;
- priority (ranking of this risk item or event against others);
- management action plans (risk response);
- manager responsible (ownership);
- result or outcome of action (updated periodically);
- date closed (for risks no longer applicable).

Table 10.2 shows an extract from a risk register for a NPD project in a pharmaceutical company where a new product cannot be launched without an information leaflet outlining dosage, side effects and other contra-indications.

There are obvious advantages to recording project risks in this way, as the risk register captures the nature of each risk in a systematic structure, with room for both quantitative analysis (ranking and overall risk scoring out of 100, by multiplying scores out of 10 for chance and impact) and qualitative analysis (text description of event, action and result). However, there are many issues in terms of how this report is used. For example, are the risk scores updated and if so by whom, how often, when was the score last updated? Is the overall risk before (raw score) or after the effect of management action (residual risk)? The other key limitation is

Table 10.2   Risk register entry

Ref.	Risk event	Chance	Impact	Overall	Rank	Action	Owner	Outcome	Closure
3.1	New product leaflet not ready on time	3	9	27	7th	Penalty clause in contract for printing	CM	Awaited, delivery est. 14 days prior to product launch	

that it appears to be systematic and comprehensive, but unless it is used wisely by people close enough to the project to fully comprehend the issues, it may be produced in a semi-automated way to give the illusion of control.

Risk registers have been in use for some time now and it would be interesting to see research into failed projects (using criteria such as cost, completion on time and perceived quality) to see just how effective the risk register was in alerting top management to problems before the project failed. As a safeguard, it may alert management to problems along the way, but only if it is taken seriously enough throughout the organization and sufficient time is devoted to sensible evaluation of the risks, rather than mechanistic or even fraudulent completion.

INTEGRATION OF RISK MANAGEMENT

Based on group discussions with participants in the logistics case organization, a model was designed in order to show how project risk assessment could be integrated with other business systems to embed risk assessment in the business planning cycle (Figure 10.1). This was partly factual and partly aspirational at the time. It was named SMART after the research project, standing for strategic management, accounting and risk techniques, which was the last in a series of action research interventions in this longitudinal case.

The main idea behind the SMART model was that strategic management and risk techniques needed to be embedded in management thinking through all six stages of the strategic planning cycle:

1. direction (strategic review – ongoing but reported annually);
2. benchmarking (quality ratings against main competitors – post bidding for contracts);
3. decisions (based on project appraisal of new business proposals);
4. learning (learning from project reviews – post-decision and implementation);

5. control (performance evaluation and management using a balanced scorecard and KPIs);
6. reporting (internal monthly management accounts, published annual reports, etc.).

Figure 10.1 shows PRAM to have the capacity to integrate steps 3 to 5 (decision-making to control) in the six-stage strategic planning cycle. This model is company specific, but follows a clockwise cycle that would be mirrored in many organizations. It is shown here to highlight the importance of integrating project risk assessment and management (PRAM) tools with other strategic processes.

The factual elements of the model in terms of the integration of PRAM are denoted by the solid red lines and the more aspirational elements are denoted by the broken red lines. Project risk assessment and management responses were considered at the decision points and at project reviews, but were only just being made known to project managers to influence project planning (using a standard software package) and performance monitoring. The aim of top management was to set and monitor KPIs that would include risk measures (emanating from the strategic level risk assessment) and link the risk dimension of project performance to corporate

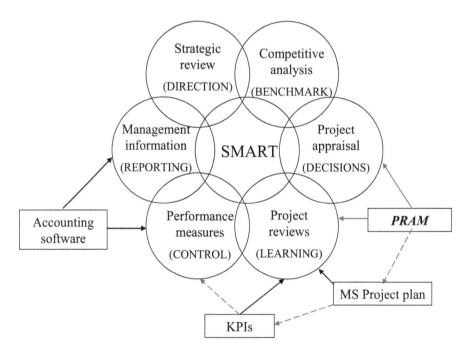

Figure 10.1   SMART model

performance. Feedback from members of other case organizations recognized this sort of linkage as a common weakness.

In many large organizations the people involved at each stage in the strategic planning cycle vary and the key conclusion from this research is that the pre-decision risk assessment information is rarely if ever passed on to the project team leader once the project implementation commences. Members of project teams are not always included in strategic planning training and development activities, so may not understand how risks have been assessed prior to strategic investment decisions. However they may well have responsibility for maintaining a project risk register, without that valuable knowledge. The link then is an issue of knowledge management, with information sharing as the key.

The theme of information sharing is continued in the next and final chapter on project reviews.

CHAPTER 11

POST-PROJECT REVIEWS

This chapter presents an argument for the re-evaluation of project risk to be an explicit part of the project review process, in order to develop organizational learning on project risk management and transfer relevant knowledge across projects. Project reviews can take place at regular intervals during a project's life cycle, but it becomes more pertinent once the project has been completed, when the outcome has been delivered and the result can be fully evaluated. In most project management literature the word risk hardly features at this stage, but the argument here is that whilst history may not repeat itself, a reflection on what the perceived risks were and how they were managed can help project managers to reduce the uncertainty involved in future projects and increase the effectiveness of project management.

PROJECT REVIEW PROCESS

The main purpose of any project review is to evaluate the project outcomes against the project aims and key success criteria. At a general level the success criteria normally cover the three traditional dimensions of project management, time, cost and quality, though additional dimensions such as the desired performance level, minimum functionality, resource efficiency, acceptability to client and users and delivery of promised benefits might also be included (Dalcher and Brodie, 2007, p. 8). Is the project (or in interim reviews the progress so far) on time, within budget and producing the desired outcome to the client's satisfaction? Whether the 'client' is internal as in some systems development projects, relocations or compliance projects, or external as in BDPs, NPDs and events, the quality criteria can be the hardest to evaluate, as it may rely on multiple perceptions and intuition rather than easily quantifiable measures. Research suggests that project reviews often focus too much on the time and cost aspects for this reason.

The review process followed usually starts with the measurement of project outcomes against success criteria. The next step is to determine what went right or wrong and for what reason, followed by an evaluation of the individual and team performance of the project team. Finally the project management process, tools and techniques are evaluated (APM, 2006, p. 90–91).

In any organization this is likely to involve a mix of rational measurement and intuitive reflection, though the latter is not always captured in project documentation (Cicmil, 2005). In examining what went right or wrong and why, managers might usefully take the project risk register as a source to inform the project team reflection and discussion. Approaches to project risk management should also be incorporated into the final stage in reviewing the effectiveness of tools and techniques used.

PROJECT REVIEW PRACTICE

Project reviews that reflect on the decision-making process as well as the project management process are rarely given sufficient time or priority in business, as the focus of management always tends to be on current issues and problems and pressing decisions (whether short-term or long-term) affecting the future. Whilst no one would advocate driving a large organization forwards using only the 'rear view mirror', many opportunities to improve future company performance are being lost by devoting insufficient time to thorough reviews.

This was recognized by participants in a recent survey (Emmanuel, Harris and Komakech, 2009), where 74 per cent of managers recognized that their organization had a post-audit evaluation (project review) stage in their strategic investment decision (SID) process, though no more than half of them said they were personally involved in it. If this cross-sectional survey is taken to be representative, it means that 26 per cent of large organizations may still have no formal project review process, and those who do may have limited managerial involvement.

Three of the 37 respondents who called for improvements to their organizations' SID process specified the need for better post-completion audits. One based these comments on an NPD project in the construction industry, one on a new site project in the beverages industry and one on a business acquisition in support services. Three respondents also called for more use of gut feel and intuition in their project appraisal process. Others highlighted risk analysis as an area for improvement. This indicates that there is certainly scope for improvement in project review practice.

INTER-PROJECT LEARNING

One of the aims of a project review is not just for the project team to learn and develop their personal project management skills, but for the organization to learn for the benefit of other project teams. Prencipe, Brady, Marshall and Tell (2005) identify several obstacles to inter-project learning, including the unique and temporary nature of projects (making learning from repetition more difficult) and organizational structures in project-based firms, where responsibility for knowledge management may not be clearly identified. This author takes the view that whilst all projects may display unique features, enough of them follow a typology, illustrated in Part 2, for inter-project learning to produce significant benefits to the firm.

A further obstacle to inter-project learning is one of corporate culture, where a blame culture will inhibit sharing of reflections. The key is to design a project review process that has three levels of analysis, individual, team and organization. Whilst individuals will naturally reflect on their own performance and achievement as part of the project team, the review process should make it 'safe' for them to share their views with others in the team, and for the team to share its conclusions with the organization, potentially through the project sponsor and through project review reporting. Whilst the methods set out in Chapter 3 are predominantly designed to help managers to identify the risks attached to specific projects, they can also be used in the project review process.

The nominal group technique is best for personal reflection, allowing each individual to garner their own thoughts about the project and its reasons for success or failure, before sharing those thoughts with the team. The repertory grid technique can aid reviews by comparing the recently completed project with others in the team members' shared experience. Finally, the cognitive maps as a visual and dynamic form of summary of project risk can be updated to aid organizational and inter-project learning. The risk map (with its underlying glossary of terms) from a specific project can be used to inform future project risk analysis of projects of similar type. Visual representations can be an efficient and effective way of transferring knowledge as they take little time to assimilate compared with text-based reports and can prompt the recipient to question and think through their own project examples.

REFLECTION ON THE PROJECT RISK APPRAISAL PROCESS

Feedback from research participants in the logistics case on the methods outlined in Chapter 2 is summarized and compared with the traditional probability impact grid (PIG) technique in Table 11.1.

The analysis in Table 11.1 (with significant text highlighted in bold) shows that the group process for project risk assessment outlined in Chapter 2 has real potential to benefit the organization as part of the project review process, so long as rationales for risk scores are captured as text entries in the spreadsheet alongside the scores.

Table 11.1   Comparative evaluation of *Pragmatix*® with a standard PIG

Probability impact grid (PIG)	*Pragmatix*®
Strengths: Better than no risk assessment Can highlight key risks Handles financial risks quite well Can be presented graphically Software widely available Can be (though often not) combined with qualitative methods	Strengths: Encourages use of intuition Designed to capture strategic risks Can be used at an early stage, pre-decision Can avoid wasted effort by screening out which invitation to tenders to respond to Provokes thought and encourages debate Brings risks and responses into the open Opportunity to benefit from full team views Assists team in understanding the risks Supported by training and user guide Uses a simple spreadsheet template Can be used to construct cognitive maps **Opportunity to link *Pragmatix*® to later project management and post audit review**
Limitations: Assumes economic rationality Subjectivity of probability and cost estimates Fails to capture ambiguity of uncertain events Often mechanistically applied Few people understand mathematical basis Often compiled by an individual Tends to exclude strategic risks Gives a false impression of exact science	Limitations: Assumes strategy is clearly understood Seen as time-consuming, especially when new teams need to establish norms Needs to be reviewed/challenged as much as DCF to avoid manipulation (by reverse engineering scores to get approval) **Insufficient text/notes to justify scores at present to be able to recall rationales at post-audit review**
Notes: The author is grateful to the members of the Project Risk Prioritisation Interest Group and the APM Risk SIG for sharing their views on the limitations of PIGs, but the author takes full responsibility for the PIG limitations expressed here	Notes: Corporate conferences provided support both to clarify strategy and introduce *Pragmatix*® Workshops provided for training new users and when new versions issued Less time-consuming after several uses **User guide was updated to overcome recall issues by adding text space to spreadsheet and updating worked examples** **Internal communications reinforced the use of *Pragmatix*® as a group exercise**

PROJECT RISK REVIEW QUESTIONS

The following questions are suggested as a checklist to guide the risk management aspects of project review and ensure project relevant knowledge is captured and passed on to future projects and project teams.

Checklist of project risk review questions:

1. What were the most significant areas of project risk (high priority risks)?
2. Was the assessment (scoring) of these project risks realistic?
3. What were the project team responses (management actions) to those risks?
4. How/did these risks impact on the project (time, quality and cost)?
5. What further action (if any) could have been taken to mitigate/exploit the risks?
6. Were there any risk factors that impacted on the project that were not included in the risk analysis?
7. If you were managing another project of this type (with similar characteristics) what would you change in the risk analysis?

The result of a project team discussion (with stakeholder representatives) guided by these questions could enhance the strategic decision-making and project management of future projects.

PROJECT RISK AND UNCERTAINTY CONCLUSIONS

This book has presented a methodology for assessing and formulating responses to strategic level project risks that can be applied to different types of projects in different organizational contexts. The application of this methodology has been illustrated for seven types of project using data from the author's research. The key skills that project managers need to be able to apply these techniques are group discussion and knowledge sharing skills such that sufficient consensus can be reached to produce a shared risk map and inform the risk management and project management systems and processes in the organization. The key to success in applying this to a variety of project scenarios and contexts is communication, so the author hopes this book will stimulate project managers to enter the discourse and share their thoughts about project risk and uncertainty in a timely way to achieve better project results.

REFERENCES

Afuah, A. 2003. *Innovation Management*. New York: Oxford University Press.

APM. 2006. *Project Management Body of Knowledge*. 5th Edition. High Wycombe: Association for Project Management.

Baccarini, D., Salm, G., and Love, P.E.D. 2004. Management of Risks in Information Technology Projects. *Industrial Management + Data Systems*, 104(3/4), pp. 286–295.

Bazerman, M. 2006. *Judgement in Managerial Decision Making*. Hoboken, NJ: John Wiley.

Bower, J.L. 1986. *Managing the Resource Allocation Process*. Boston, Mass.: Harvard Business School Press.

Bromwich, M. 1976. *The Economics of Capital Budgeting*. London: Penguin.

Carter, B., Hancock, T., Morin, J.-M. and Robins, N. 1994. *Introducing RISKMAN Methodology*. Oxford: Blackwell.

Cassell, C. and Walsh, S. 2004. Repertory Grids, in *Essential Guide to Qualitative Methods in Organizational Research*, edited by C. Cassell and G. Symon. London: Sage, pp. 61–72.

Cicmil, S. 2005. Reflection, participation and learning in project environments: A multiple perspective agenda, In *Management of Knowledge in Project Environments*, edited by P.E.D. Love, P.S.W. Fong and Z. Irani. Oxford: Elsevier, pp. 155–180.

Chapman, C. and Ward, S. 2003. *Project Risk Management: Processes, Techniques and Insights*. Chichester: John Wiley.

Collier, P., Berry, A.J. and Burke, G.T. 2007. *Risk and Management Accounting: Best Practice Guidelines for Enterprise-wide Internal Control Procedures*. Oxford: Elsevier.

Crawford, L., Hobbs, B., and Turner, J.R. 2006. Aligning Capability with Strategy: Categorizing Projects to Do the Right Projects and to Do Them Right. *Project Management Journal*, 37(2), pp. 38–50.

Dalcher, D. and Brodie, L. 2007. *Successful IT Projects*. London: Thomson Learning.

Delbecq, A.L., Van de Ven, A.H. and Gustafson, D.H. 1975. *Group Techniques for Program Planning: A Guide to Nominal Group and Delphi Processes*. Glenview, Illinois: Scott Foresman.

Dunbar, W.S. 2007. Perceptions of Risk in the Mining Industry, *International Journal of Risk Assessment and Management,* 7(5), pp. 722–738.

Eden, C. 1988. Cognitive Mapping: A Review. *European Journal of Operational Research,* 36, pp. 1–13.

Eden, C. and Simpson, P. 1989. SODA and cognitive mapping in practice, In *Rational Analysis for a Problematic World,* edited by J. Rosenhead. Chichester: John Wiley, pp. 43–70.

Edkins, A.J., Kurul, E., Maytorena-Sanchez, E. and Rintala, K. 2007. The Application of Cognitive Mapping Methodologies in Project Management Research. *International Journal of Project Management,* 25, pp. 762–772.

Emery, P.R. 2002. Bidding to Host a Major Sports Event: The Local Organising Committee Perspective. *The International Journal of Public Sector Management,* 15(4/5), pp. 316–335.

Emmanuel, C.R., Harris, E.P. and Komakech, S. 2009. *Managerial Judgement and Strategic Investment Decisions: A Cross-sectional Survey.* Oxford: Elsevier.

Fransella, F. and Bannister, D. 1977. *A Manual for Repertory Grid Technique.* London: Academic Press.

Gilovich, T., Griffin, D., and Kahneman, D. (eds) 2002. *Heuristics and Biases: The Psychology of Intuitive Judgement.* New York: Cambridge University Press.

Harris, E. 1999. Project Risk Assessment: A European Field Study. *British Accounting Review,* 31(3), pp. 347–371.

Harris, E.P. 2007. How Managers Construe Risk in Business Acquisitions. *International Journal of Risk Assessment and Management,* 7(8), forthcoming.

Harris, E. and Woolley, R. 2009. Facilitating Innovation Through Cognitive Mapping of Uncertainty. *International Studies of Management and Organization,* 39(1), pp. 71–100.

Hastie, R. and Dawes, R. 2001. *Rational Choice in an Uncertain World.* Thousand Oaks: Sage.

Helliar, C.V., Lonie, A.A., Power, D.M. and Sinclair, C.D. 2001. *Attitudes of UK Managers to Risk and Uncertainty.* Institute of Chartered Accountants of Scotland, Glasgow.

Hillson, D. and Murray-Webster, R. 2005. *Understanding and Managing Risk Attitude.* Aldershot: Gower.

Hopkinson, M., Close, P., Hillson, D. and Ward, S. (eds) 2008. *Prioritising Project Risks: A Short Guide to Useful Techniques.* Princes Risborough: APM Publishing.

Huff, A.S. and Jenkins, M. (eds) 2002. *Mapping Strategic Knowledge.* London: Sage.

Johnson, P. and Johnson, G. 2002. Facilitating group cognitive mapping of core competences, In *Mapping Strategic Knowledge,* edited by A.S. Huff and M. Jenkins) London: Sage, pp. 220–236.

Johnson, G. and Scholes, K. 1993. *Exploring Corporate Strategy: Text and Cases.* 3rd Edition. Hemel Hempstead: Prentice Hall.

Kahneman, D. and Tversky, A. 1979. Prospect Theory: An Analysis of Decision Under Risk. *Econometrica,* 47(2), pp. 263–291.

Kelly, G.A. 1955. *The Psychology of Personal Constructs.* New York: Norton.

King, P. 1975. Is the Emphasis of Capital Budgeting Theory Misplaced? *Journal of Business Finance and Accounting,* 2(1), pp. 69–82.

Langfield-Smith, K. 2005. What do we know about management control systems and strategy?, In *Controlling Strategy,* edited by C.S. Chapman. New York: Oxford University Press, pp. 62–85.

Mendelow, A. 1991. *Proceedings of 2nd International Conference on Information Systems.* Cambridge, Massachusetts, cited by G. Johnson and K. Scholes 1993. *Exploring Corporate Strategy: Text and Cases.* 3rd Edition. Hemel Hempstead: Prentice Hall, p. 177.

Mintzberg, H.D., Raisinghani, D. and Theoret, A. 1976. The Structure of Unstructured Decision Processes. *Administrative Science Quarterly,* 21(2), pp. 246–275.

PMI 2008. *A Guide to the Project Management Body of Knowledge.* 4th Edition *(PMBOK® Guide).* Pennsylvania: Project Management Institute.

Prencipe, A., Brady, T., Marshall, N., and Tell, F. 2005. Making sense of learning landscapes in project-based organizations, In *Management of Knowledge in Project Environments,* edited by P.E.D. Love P.S.W. Fong and Z. Irani. Oxford: Elsevier, pp. 197–218.

Rugg, G. and McGeorge, P. 1995. Laddering. *Expert Systems,* 12(4), pp. 339–346.

Rugg, G. and Shadbolt, N.R. 1991. On the Limitations of Repertory Grids in Knowledge Acquisition, in *6th BanFF Knowledge Acquisition for Knowledge-Based Systems Workshop,* Vol. 2 BanFF, Canada, 22-1 to 22-17.

Simon, H.A. 1947, 1957, 1976. *Administrative Behaviour: A Study of Decision-Making Processes in Administrative Organization.* New York: Macmillan.

Slovic, P. 2000. *The Perception of Risk.* London: Earthscan.

Slovic, P., Finucane, M., Peters, E. and MacGregor, D.G. 2002. The affect heuristic, In *Heuristics and Biases: The Psychology of Intuitive Judgement,* edited by Gilovich, Griffin and Kahneman. New York: Cambridge University Press, pp. 397–420.

Tversky, A. and Kahneman, D. 1981. The Framing of Decisions and the Psychology of Choice. *Science,* pp. 453–458.

Tesch, D., Kloppenborg, T.J. and Frolick, M.N. 2007. IT Project Risk Factors: The Project Management Profession Perspective. *Journal of Computer Information Systems,* 47(4), pp. 61–69.

Webb, A. 2003. *The Project Manager's Guide to Handling Risk.* Aldershot: Gower.

Williams, T., Ackermann, F., Eden, C. and Howick, S. 2005. Learning from project failure, In *Management of Knowledge in Project Environments,* edited by P.E.D. Love, P.S.W. Fong and Z. Irani. Oxford: Elsevier, pp. 219–236.

Woolley, R. 2005. *Managing Innovation Through Cognitive Mapping.* Unpublished PhD thesis. Leicester: De Montfort University.

INDEX

FUNDAMENTALS OF PROJECT MANAGEMENT and ADVANCES IN PROJECT MANAGEMENT

Project management has become a key competence for most organisations in the public and private sectors. Driven by recent business trends such as fewer management layers, greater flexibility, increasing geographical distribution and more project-based work, project management has grown beyond its roots in the construction, engineering and aerospace industries to transform the service, financial, computer, and general management sectors. In fact, a *Fortune* article rated project management as the number one career choice at the beginning of the 21st century.

Yet many organisations have struggled in applying the traditional models of project management to their new projects in the global environment. Project management offers a framework to help organisations to transform their mainstream operations and service performance. It is viewed as a way of organising for the future. Moreover, in an increasingly busy, stressful, and uncertain world it has become necessary to manage several projects successfully at the same time. According to some estimates the world annually spends well over $10 trillion (US) on projects. In the UK alone, more than £250 billion is spent on projects every year. Up to half of these projects fail! A major ingredient in the build-up leading to failure is often cited as the lack of adequate project management knowledge and experience.

Some organizations have responded to this situation by trying to improve the understanding and capability of their managers and employees who are introduced to projects, as well as their experienced project managers in an attempt to enhance their competence and capability in this area.

FUNDAMENTALS OF PROJECT MANAGEMENT SERIES

This series of short guides covers the key aspects of project management: Benefits Management; Business Case; Change Management; Cost Management; Financing; Governance; Leadership; Organization; Program Management; Progress Management/Earned Value; Planning; Quality Management; Risk Management; Scope; Scheduling; Sponsorship; Stakeholder Management; Value Management.

Each guide, as the series title suggests, aims to provide the fundamentals of the subject from a rigorous perspective and from a leading proponent of the subject.

Visit: www.gowerpublishing.com/fundamentalsofprojectmanagement for more information and a list of titles

ADVANCES IN PROJECT MANAGEMENT

Advances in Project Management provides short, state of play, guides to the main aspects of the new emerging applications of project management including: maturity models, agile projects, extreme projects, six sigma and projects, human factors and leadership in projects, project governance, value management, virtual teams, project benefits.

Visit www.gowerpublishing.com/advancesinprojectmanagement for more information and a list of titles.

EDITOR FOR BOTH SERIES:

Professor Darren Dalcher is Director of the National Centre for Project Management, a Professor of Software Project Management at Middlesex University and Visiting Professor of Computer Science at the University of Iceland.

National Centre for Project Management Middlesex University College House Trent Park Bramley Road London N14 4YZ United Kingdom Email: ncpm@mdx. ac.uk Phone: +44 (0)20 8411 2299 Fax no. +44 (0)20 8411 5133